Instant Pot®
Miracle
VEGETARIAN
COOKBOOK

Instant Pot®
Miracle
VEGETARIAN
COOKBOOK

More Than 100 Easy Meatless Meals
for Your Favorite Kitchen Device

URVASHI PITRE

PHOTOGRAPHY BY GHAZALLE BADIOZAMANI

HOUGHTON MIFFLIN HARCOURT
BOSTON NEW YORK 2020

For information about permission to reproduce selections from this book, write to trade.permissions@hmhco.com or to Permissions, Houghton Mifflin Harcourt Publishing Company, 3 Park Avenue, 19th Floor, New York, New York 10016.

hmhbooks.com

Library of Congress Cataloging-in-Publication Data

Names: Pitre, Urvashi, author. | Badiozamani, Ghazalle (Photographer), photographer,

Title: Instant pot miracle vegetarian cookbook : more than 100 easy meatless meals for your favorite kitchen device / Urvashi Pitre ; photography by Ghazalle Badiozamani.

Description: Boston : Houghton Mifflin Harcourt, 2020. | Includes index. | Identifiers: LCCN 2020009486 (print) | LCCN 2020009487 (ebook) | ISBN 9780358379331 (trade paperback) | ISBN 9780358378846 (ebook)

Subjects: LCSH: Vegetarian cooking. | Quick and easy cooking. | Smart cookers. | Pressure cooking. | Electric cooking. | LCGFT: Cookbooks.

Classification: LCC TX837 .P576 2020 (print) | LCC TX837 (ebook) | DDC 641.5/636—dc23

LC record available at https://lccn.loc.gov/2020009486

LC ebook record available at https://lccn.loc.gov/2020009487

Book design by Jennifer K. Beal Davis

Printed in China

SCP 10 9 8 7 6 5 4 3 2 1

To my husband, Roger,
who is my best friend
and my staunchest advocate.
I couldn't do any of this
without you.

CONTENTS

VEGETABLES

LENTILS, BEANS & LEGUMES

RICE & GRAINS

EGGS & CHEESE

DESSERTS & DRINKS

SAUCES & SPICE MIXES

ACKNOWLEDGMENTS

My biggest thanks go to my fans, followers, and readers, who continue to support, suggest, encourage, and make me laugh daily. If it weren't for you, I'd be creating recipes that absolutely no one made—and how little fun would that be?

My husband, who continues to eat all my successes and failures and gives me honest feedback no matter what.

Sheila Ward, who helped me painstakingly test every recipe in this book, some of them more than once.

Sammy and Paul Brakebill and Ashley Reachelle, who help me keep twosleevers.com going when I'm in the throes of recipe creation.

Lisa Kingsley and Will Bortz for rewriting the recipes for clarity.

My agent, Stacey Glick, who is always available when I need her, and who supports me in so many ways.

My editor, Justin Schwartz, whose involvement and input really help these books come together.

Ghazalle Badiozamani and her team of accomplished stylists and helpers, who make my food look pretty—not just tasty. Thank you to Monica Pierini, Jenna Tedesco, and Bridget Kenny for your great work. I so love working with you.

Thanks also to Bridget Nocera and Samantha Simon, who help me brainstorm crazy publicity and marketing ideas, as well as the whole army at Houghton Mifflin Harcourt that helped, without my even realizing it, make this book a reality.

INTRODUCTION

I have been cooking with pressure cookers for over thirty-five years. (I feel old just writing that! Let's just assume I started cooking at two years old, okay?) My relationship with them has evolved. Just as in other long-term relationships, over the years I have loved them, used them, taken them for granted during busy times, explored their capabilities during times of rest, understood their giving nature better, and fallen in love with them again.

About five years ago, I discovered the world of electric pressure cookers. Soon after, the Instant Pot entered my life, and slowly, it took over my kitchen. In fact, as my life was taken over by a degenerative disease that often limited my mobility, I began to rely more and more on these devices that allowed me to cook a quick, nutritious dinner without babysitting, standing, stirring, and mixing.

My husband, Roger, and I were also on a weight-loss journey, and home-cooked meals were critical in this endeavor. Together, we have lost and kept off about 175 pounds, and cooking healthy meals at home was an important part of how we accomplished this feat.

My son Mark learned to cook with a pressure cooker when he was nineteen years old. I still remember when he mastered four different dishes in one day. Now, Mark is scary-smart, this is true, but it's also true that pressure cookers are not that complicated.

I want to use this book, my blog (twosleevers.com), and my Facebook groups as a way to introduce you to the delights of cooking in a pressure cooker. I assure you, once you realize all that it can do, you may well find the other appliances in your kitchen, along with your stove, becoming sorely neglected.

If you are a novice cook, forget all your fears, your concerns, and your confusion. Just pick a recipe from this book—any recipe—and make it by following the simple directions. Through the pages of this book, I'll help you create amazing meals. Just like the thousands before you who never cooked but now make my recipes nightly, you, too, can do this. If you are an accomplished cook already, you may enjoy the different shortcuts I use, as well as appreciate the wide range of flavors and cuisines covered in this book.

There's something for everyone in this recipe book. I hope you enjoy it. If you run into issues, do be sure to ask me questions on my blog, twosleevers.com, or come join my TwoSleevers Facebook group, facebook.com/twosleever, which is filled with helpful, kind folks ready to lend a hand.

WELCOME TO MEATLESS MEALS

I grew up eating largely vegetarian meals. For the first twenty-plus years of my life, we ate meat maybe once a week, if that. This was quite normal for most of us in India, a country that is predominantly vegetarian, even today.

This is why I was quite surprised when I polled my TwoSleevers Facebook group and got the following feedback about vegetarian food from the group members. When asked what concerns they had about buying an Instant Pot vegetarian cookbook, here's what they were concerned about:

- Use of "pseudo meats" in the recipes
- Not enough protein in the food
- Too much reliance on tofu or other processed foods
- Not really whole/real foods
- Meals might not be very filling (think light salads and veggies only)

Let's cut to the chase. This book should set all those fears to rest.

- There are no pseudo meats or meat substitutes.
- There is a lot of protein in beans and other natural sources.
- Tofu is used in only three recipes where you would traditionally find it (kimchi jiggae, hot-and-sour soup, and as an option in congee).
- As with all my other cookbooks, I use whole, unprocessed ingredients as much as possible. I do not ask you to use canned soups or prepackaged mixes.

What Ingredients Will I Need?

There are a few ingredients you'll want to stock up on. This is not an exhaustive list of everything used in the book; rather, it's a listing of some ingredients that omnivores may or may not have in their pantries. You should know that I absolutely hate buying an ingredient to use in just one recipe, so in most cases, these ingredients are used in more than one recipe in this book. Also note that you do not need to run out and buy all these at once. Just look at the recipes and see what sounds good, and then you can decide what you have to have right away.

Rice & Grains

Arborio rice

Basmati rice

Black rice

Brown rice

Bulgur

Couscous

Dried hominy

Farina

Glutinous rice

Jasmine rice

Kasha/toasted buckwheat groats

Millet

Pearled barley

Pearled farro

Quinoa

Short-grain rice

Wild rice blend

Beans

Adzuki beans

Black beans

Black-eyed peas

Brown lentils

Cannellini beans

Chickpeas

15-bean mix

French lentils

Gigantes beans

Lima beans

Kidney beans

Mung beans

Navy beans

Pinto beans

Red beans

Red lentils

Split moong dal

See what I mean? Whole foods. Things that are both yummy and good for you. No "franken-ingredients."

THE RECIPES IN THIS BOOK

Very Easy

If you can chop, mix, blend, stir, and press buttons, you can make these dishes. So, yes, your fourteen-year-old can likely make most of this food. The recipes were designed to be easy for the average home chef—you know, the real people like me who don't have caviar, octopus, and that certain truffle that only grows in the Alps just lying around in their pantry. Many of these recipes use pantry and freezer vegetables, but not canned cream-of-anything soups or ready-made sauces in cans. Having said that, I do like to cook recipes from around the world. There are recipes that may call for ingredients you don't currently have.

Authentic Recipes from Around the World

You may not be familiar with all the cuisines and taste profiles I feature in this book. But here's your chance to try something different, while relying on recipes that are extremely well tested and whose flavors have been blessed by those who grew up eating or cooking these dishes from around the world. My very active Facebook group is filled with foodies, many of whom are well-traveled and accomplished cooks. They helped vet the ease and authenticity of all these recipes.

I urge you to step out of your usual cooking rut or your comfort zone with some of these recipes, and do so with the expectation that you and your family may find flavors that become your new favorites. My advice to you is that you not tell yourself, "Oh, but I don't like [insert cuisine here]." Rather, look at a recipe and its ingredients. Does it have flavors you enjoy? If so, try making the recipe. Nine times out of ten, my readers who do this end up raving about a hitherto-unheard-of dish. Of course, if you hate mushrooms, you're unlikely to enjoy them in any dish, no matter the cuisine. So be a little brave, but use what you know about your tastes to pick and choose.

Thoroughly Tested

Every recipe in this book has been tested not just by me but also by several people in my TwoSleevers Facebook group, as well as by readers of my blog. If a recipe doesn't work for you, it's unlikely to be the recipe and more likely to be something that you could do differently. Make each recipe once as written and then feel free to experiment. If you're still having issues, please ask questions on my blog or in my Facebook group, and someone will help you.

I tested (and retested!) all the Instant Pot recipes in either a 6-quart Duo, 6-quart Ultra, or 3-quart Mini Instant Pot. Each model has its own nuances, so I've tried to keep the instructions as generic as possible. These recipes work as written in a 6-quart Instant Pot. All but the ones that require pot-in-pot cooking also work in a 3-quart model. If you're using an 8-quart Instant Pot, you may need to add ¼ cup water to recipes that do not call for added water.

Customizable

It's very easy to customize many of the dishes by using the beans or grains of your choice. As long as you substitute like-size beans for each other (in other words, don't substitute giant-size dried lima beans for fine split lentils and assume the same cook times still apply), you should be okay. The lentil and rice chapters contain introductions that will give you cook times for various rice and beans to help you substitute.

Leverage the Science of Pressure Cooking

I am a scientist by training. Not for nothing do I have a doctorate in experimental psychology. I am also a gadget geek, as you can see from my various Instant Pot and air-fryer cookbooks. I believe in thoroughly understanding a gadget and how it works, and then leveraging it to cook differently.

These recipes skip many of the steps that you use in stovetop or oven cooking, such as browning meat or vegetables. The pressure cooker is capable of browning your food for you (watch my video about the Maillard reaction in a pressure cooker on my blog or YouTube channel). I spent a long time testing and streamlining recipes so that you don't have to. I'll urge you to do what my groups do, which is to #trustUrvashi and try a recipe as written the first time. You can tweak it to your preference the next time around.

Leverage the Power of the Instant Pot

When I buy an Instant Pot cookbook with recipes that require me to sauté on the stovetop, bake in the oven, and/or fry in an air fryer, and then cook in the Instant Pot—all for one dish sometimes—I am driven mad. Very few dishes in this cookbook require this type of "You must surely have elves to wash all hundred pots you just dirtied" type of cooking. Most are made entirely in the Instant Pot, with some recipes suggesting different ways you can finish them off.

Unleash Your Inner Kitchen God or Goddess (or Both)

I see my job as equipping you with the basics you need to cook—and then encouraging you to tweak the recipes so you can make your own adaptations. Trust me when I tell you that inside you, there is a kitchen god or goddess waiting to be unleashed. All he or she needs is a little love and a little knowledge. I am very sure that as you work your way through these recipes, your confidence will grow, your lucky dinner guests will enjoy your cooking, and you'll start to see yourself as an accomplished cook, even if you have never cooked elaborate meals before.

WHY INSTANT POT?

The Instant Pot combines several kitchen appliances in one: pressure cooker, rice cooker, slow cooker, yogurt maker, and sterilizer. Some models can even cook sous vide. But for most people, its most popular function is pressure cooking. A pressure cooker changes the boiling point of water. In the sealed cooking environment, the steam generated by boiling liquid can't escape, so it builds up and creates pressure. As the pressure increases, the boiling point of water is raised. In the Instant Pot, a high pressure of 11.6 psi (pounds per square inch) can raise the boiling point of water from 212°F (100°C) to 245°F (118°C). This cooks foods faster and thus retains more flavor. Cooking under pressure infuses food with flavor in a way stovetop cooking can't match.

Speed

The Instant Pot speeds up cooking by two to six times, making it extremely energy-efficient, while preserving nutrients and resulting in healthy, tasty dishes. This is especially true for tough grains and beans. The Instant Pot is the fastest, easiest, most foolproof way to get these done.

Tough beans like chickpeas and kidney beans can be prepared in about thirty minutes under pressure and, best of all, require no stirring or watching over the dish as it cooks. Fresh or frozen green peas, sweet corn, and baby carrots can be steamed in two to three minutes. For mashed potatoes, there is no longer a need to boil the potatoes in water for thirty minutes—instead, steam them for only fifteen minutes.

Hands-Off Cooking

Hands-off cooking is what most people find so appealing about cooking with an Instant Pot. Once you place your food in it and set the appropriate cooking time, you can be assured that the food will cook as it should and you'll be presented with a tasty meal when it's done. What's more, your meal will be kept warm until you're ready to eat.

Better Nutrition and Taste

The fully sealed environment of the Instant Pot traps the flavors, nutrients, and aromas of the food, instead of releasing them throughout your home. Heat is distributed evenly, deeply, and quickly once pressure builds up. Minimal water is required for steaming, so vitamins and minerals are not leached or dissolved. Greens retain their bright colors and whole grains and beans are perfectly tender and delicious.

Cooking under pressure infuses food with flavor in a way stovetop cooking can't match. When I try the same recipe on the stovetop and in an Instant Pot, the difference is remarkable.

No, It's Not Actually "Instant"

I have tried hard to list reasonable prep and cooking times for the recipes in this book. The total time for a recipe also includes the time it takes for your pot to come to pressure, as well as for the pressure to be released. In this book, we assume ten minutes for the pot to come to pressure. Total cook time is prep time, plus ten minutes for the pot to come to pressure, plus cooking time under pressure, plus the pressure release time.

The first time you make a recipe, allow thirty to forty-five minutes for the entire process, even if a recipe says it cooks in fifteen minutes under pressure. How long it takes for the pot to come to pressure is controlled by many factors:

- How much food is in the pot: A fuller pot takes longer to come to pressure.
- Whether the food was frozen when you started: While cooking time under pressure will be the same, the time it takes to build pressure will be longer with frozen foods.

- How much liquid you have in the pot: More liquid means it takes longer to build pressure. This is why some of my recipes ask you to use very little water up front, but then say to thin the dish with water after cooking to reach the right consistency.

No Need to Sauté for Browning

One of the most common mistakes people make when cooking with or writing recipes for a pressure cooker is to brown foods excessively before cooking under pressure. I have created a video on twosleevers.com about how the pressure cooker encourages the Maillard reaction without the need to brown foods ahead of time. It's quite nerdy and geeky, but hopefully also informative—kinda like me! So stop browning your meats ahead of time, and just let the pressure cooker do the work for you. And stop evaporating the flavorful liquids out of vegetables and then adding plain water to compensate. Just cook these dishes like I ask you to and you can save time and effort while leveraging the pressure cooker's abilities.

An Unwatched Pot

Once the pot is sealed, there's no need to watch the beans and test them repeatedly to prevent undercooking, or to stir continuously to keep things from burning. If you're like me and easily distracted by shiny objects, you'll find the Instant Pot to be a blessing.

Heat Efficiency and Odors

Not leaving your oven on for hours, not heating up your kitchen, and not having smells permeate your house can be a wonderful thing. Not having to turn on your oven to make a cake is a really wonderful thing, especially during the summer.

Cooking on the Road and in Dorms or Apartments

Many people use their Instant Pots while traveling, while camping in RVs, in boats, in hotel rooms, in smaller apartments, and in dorms, all situations where there might not be access to multiple appliances, ovens, or large amounts of counter space. The ability to multitask is a huge advantage of this multicooker.

INSTANT POT TERMS TO KNOW AND WHEN TO USE THEM

PIP (Pot-in-Pot) Cooking

This refers to the practice of using a trivet or steamer rack and an additional heatproof pan to cook multiple dishes or components in the Instant Pot at the same time. Typically, one dish is cooked directly in the pot, while the other is cooked in a separate smaller pan that rests on the trivet.

In some cases, you will place water in the inner liner of the Instant Pot to generate steam. You may also be asked to place water inside the small heatproof pot that holds the ingredients being cooked, such as beans, rice, etc. If you are only steaming vegetables lightly, you may not be required to put water into the smaller pan.

A simple rule of thumb is that anything that absorbs water while cooking (rice, beans, pasta, potatoes, and other starches) requires added water. Anything that releases water, like most nonstarchy vegetables, doesn't require water to cook, but may benefit from broths and sauces to add flavor.

NPR (Natural Pressure Release) and QPR (Quick Pressure Release)

Once the Instant Pot has finished the cook cycle, it will beep to let you know. At this point, most recipes direct you to release pressure naturally, quickly release the pressure, or sometimes to use a combination of the two, such as allowing the pot to release pressure naturally for ten minutes and then quickly releasing the remaining pressure.

NPR: To release pressure naturally, simply allow the pot to rest undisturbed after the cook cycle has finished. As it cools, it will gradually release pressure until the float valve drops, indicating that the pot is no longer under pressure. You do not need to turn off the Keep Warm feature to enable NPR. The pot will drop both temperature and pressure on its own and move to the Keep Warm setting (unless you've expressly disabled it), allowing you to enjoy your dinner when you're ready. The short version is, NPR = do nothing and wait patiently for the pin to drop.

QPR: To release pressure quickly, press down on the button on top of the lid or turn the dial on the steam valve to Venting. This allows the pot to release steam and pressure. Ensure that the pot is not directly under cabinets that may be damaged by the hot steam, and be sure to keep your hands and face away from the steam. Do not allow children to "help" with this.

What Are All These Buttons and Do I Really Need Them All?

Even though I have been using my Instant Pot for years, I do understand the bewilderment that accompanies the acquisition of a new Instant Pot. There are so many buttons! Standing in front of your new Instant Pot, you stare at the control panel, wondering if you're about to cook dinner or launch a rocket. The instrument panel has stopped many a hungry person in her tracks, but I'm going to make this very easy for you.

In this book, almost all the recipes use just two settings: Sauté, plus Pressure Cook (for those with the Ultra model) or Manual (for those with the Duo or Lux models). Those are the only settings you need to cook most of these recipes.

Having said that, it's good to understand what the other settings do. (If you're more of a visual learner, I have a video on this topic on my blog.) It's a common misperception that all the settings are really the same, just programmed with different times. Many—but not all—of the buttons are unique in some combination of time, pressure, and temperature. According to my testing, there are six settings that have specific functions rather than just different time programs, as I've detailed below.

Understanding the Six Most Important Buttons on Your Instant Pot

There can be as many as sixteen buttons on the Instant Pot, broken down as follows: The pressure-cook programs include Ultra, Pressure Cook, Meat/Stew, Soup/Broth, Bean/Chili, Steam, Sterilize, Rice, Multigrain, Porridge, Egg, and Cake. The non-pressure-cook programs include Slow Cook, Sauté, Warm, and Yogurt.

Sauté: This functions exactly like a pan on the stovetop to brown and sear, and you can set it to High, Medium, or Low temperatures. This is not pressure cooking, just heating and browning.

Pressure Cook/Manual: This will likely be your most often used button. The buttons usually default to High pressure, and you can set the cooking time. When a recipe says, "Set to HIGH pressure for 5 minutes," for example, this is the button you'll reach for, and then you'll likely use the +/− buttons (or a dial) to set the cooking time to five minutes.

Soup: When you use the Soup button, the pressure cooker heats up very slowly at first, before hitting higher temperatures. It was originally designed to create noncloudy broths for soups. I find it quite useful when you are trying to keep yogurt or other liquids from separating.

Steam: Confusingly, it's called Steam, but it's under pressure. When you use this button, the pot raises its temperature very quickly—and it stays hot. This allows your food to cook very quickly, without a longer lead time before the pot comes to pressure. This is very useful when you're cooking delicate items such as vegetables. You must, however, use a steamer rack if you use the Steam function. Do not place food directly on the bottom of the pot, or it will likely scorch.

Yogurt: Making yogurt at home ensures that you know exactly what went into it and allows you to customize it to better suit your family's tastes. I also use this function to sprout beans and to proof bread dough. One caveat, though: Do not use the Instant Pot lid when proofing dough. Use a glass lid or other easily removable lid. If your bread rises a little too enthusiastically, you may find the lid stuck tight with no easy way to remove it.

Slow Cook: There are many debates as to whether an Instant Pot can slow cook well. My experience suggests that it can—with a caveat. Forget everything you know about settings on a slow cooker, because the Instant Pot has settings of its own:

- Low on an Instant Pot = Warm on a regular slow cooker
- Medium on an Instant Pot = Low on a regular slow cooker
- High on an Instant Pot = High on a regular slow cooker

If this confusing, just remember—don't use the Low setting to cook. Use either Medium or High, and you'll be fine. I suggest you try your first slow-cooked recipe on a day you'll be at home, rather than at the end of a long day at work, so you're not adding confusion and frustration to hunger.

You can leave the steam vent open or closed when you slow cook.

Pressure Cooking at High Altitudes

The higher the altitude, the lower the atmospheric pressure. In cooking, this means that the higher the altitude, the lower the boiling point of water (and other liquids), and the faster water evaporates. When you get above an altitude of 2,000 feet above sea level, the difference can be significant. While the sealed interior of a pressure cooker helps make up for the lower atmospheric pressure, you'll still have to make some adjustments if you live in the mountains and are using any model of the Instant Pot other than the Ultra.

Most pressure cooker manufacturers recommend increasing cooking times by 5 percent for every 1,000 feet above 2,000 feet, so a dish that cooks under pressure for 20 minutes at sea level would cook for 21 minutes at 3,000 feet or 22 minutes at 4,000 feet. Some manufacturers also recommend increasing the amount of liquid slightly.

If you have the Instant Pot Ultra, there's no need to adjust cooking times. This model allows you to specify your altitude up to 9,900 feet, and the machine will adjust cooking times accordingly.

FREQUENTLY ASKED QUESTIONS

I often post Instant Pot recipes on my blog, twosleevers.com, as well as on my Facebook pages and groups, and I always get lots of comments and feedback, which I love. While most people quickly master a few recipes, many wish to do even more with the appliance. Even though it's my priority to create easy, simple recipes, I still want those recipes to help you explore and enjoy your appliance, as well as expand your palate. Here is a collection of some of the questions I get asked most often, and my answers to help you on your journey as you cook with the Instant Pot.

Equipment Questions

My pot is spitting steam.

Note where the steam appears to be coming from. If it's coming from the valve, it's not unusual for the pot to release a little steam as it comes up to pressure, and once the valve floats up and seals, it should stop leaking steam. If, however, you're getting a steady flow of stream from the sealing ring, the seal is not tight or may need replacing. In this case, the pot will not come to pressure. Turn it off, and reset or replace the seal.

My lid won't open.

If your lid won't open, the pot is likely under pressure. Do not force it! Wait for all the pressure to be released before you try again. Forcing it can result in serious burns and injuries. If you've been waiting for twenty-five to thirty minutes and it still won't open, and the float valve is still up, it's possible something is stuck under the valve. Very carefully, using a long-handled spoon or fork, gently tap the float valve. This is usually enough to get the valve to drop. Clean the lid and the valve carefully before you begin the next cooking cycle.

My lid won't close.

If your lid won't close, the most likely culprit is the sealing ring. Remove it and reinsert it following the directions that came with the Instant Pot. Ensure there is no food or debris lodged in the sides of the lid or the rim of the pot. Ensure that the liner you're using is the correct one.

The second most common reason is that you've opened the pot and decided you needed to cook the food a little longer, but now the lid won't go back on easily. The steam in the pot often pushes the valve up in these situations. Turn the float valve to Venting to allow some of that steam to dissipate and try again.

I've been waiting forever for the pin to drop, but it says it's still locked.

Hmm . . . "forever" is kinda relative, isn't it? Okay, jokes aside, realize that a very full pot, especially one filled with liquid, takes longer to come to pressure and longer to release pressure. If you're sure you've given it plenty of time on its own, the float valve may be stuck. Very carefully, using a long-handled spoon or fork, gently tap the float valve. This is usually enough to get the valve to drop. Clean the lid and the valve carefully before the next cooking cycle.

My sealing ring smells like the last savory thing I cooked. How do I get rid of the odor?

A few things work to keep the sealing ring from retaining odors:

- Remove and wash it each time, but don't forget to put it back before cooking again!
- Prop the lid on the side of the pot to allow both pot and lid to air out.
- Odd though it may sound, soaking the ring in a sink full of water along with a denture-cleaning tablet is quite effective.
- Wash the ring well and put it out in the sun to dry. This method is highly effective, but, of course, quite impractical on a dreary winter day.

General Food Questions

Why is my food under-/overcooked?

The most common reasons for under- or overcooked food are:

- Insufficient water in the Instant Pot (undercooked)
- Pieces of food were larger (undercooked)/smaller (overcooked) than what the recipe called for

- Doing NPR when the recipe calls for QPR (overcooked), or QPR when the recipe calls for NPR (undercooked)

Why does my food keep burning?

The most common reasons for burning are:

- Insufficient water in the Instant Pot
- Substituting ingredients that absorb water (e.g., potatoes, pasta, rice, grains, beans, and legumes) for ingredients that release water (e.g., most meats and vegetables) in the recipe
- Food stuck to the bottom of the pot while sautéing (I cannot overemphasize the necessity of deglazing thoroughly in an Instant Pot)
- Thick liquids, such as tomato sauces, thick cream soups, etc., being used to bring the pot to pressure. If you must use these thick liquids, use plain water at the bottom, then add the meat or vegetables, and layer the thick liquids on top without stirring.
- Inadequate seal causing water to evaporate

I thought we had to have 1 cup of water for the Instant Pot to come to pressure. How is it that your recipes often have no added water?

You do need water for the Instant Pot to come to pressure, but I prefer to get that water directly from the ingredients rather than adding tap water. Most vegetables release a lot of water as they cook. This flavorful broth seasons the dish better than tap water. It also keeps you from having to boil away the excess water at the end, which can result in an overcooked dish. Pressure cooking imparts a better taste because it keeps your meal from being boiled as it cooks. Using the Sauté function to boil excess water defeats that purpose.

Note, however, that rice, beans, lentils, and other legumes do require water to cook. They absorb water and swell (and foam) as they cook. But they require a lot less water when cooked in an Instant Pot than they do cooked on the stovetop. This is largely because on a stovetop, you lose most of the water through evaporation. In a contained and sealed environment, water loss is kept to a minimum. Use the water amounts specified in these recipes and in pressure-cooking charts for best results.

I used my Slow Cook function, but hours later my food is still raw. Why?

Your Instant Pot is a fully functional slow cooker that is capable of producing delicious slow-cooked meals. If you have been using a traditional slow cooker, the following maybe helpful for you.

- The Low setting should be used to keep foods warm, not to cook foods.
- The Medium setting functions much like the Low setting on a traditional slow cooker. Use the Medium setting for slow cooking.
- The High setting functions much like the High setting on a traditional slow cooker. Use this setting for slightly faster slow cooking.

Yogurt Questions

I left my yogurt in for longer than eight hours. Is it spoiled?

Yogurt can be left to incubate safely for 12 to 14 hours. After that, it will not spoil, but it might be more tart than you prefer. The longer it incubates, the more tart it will taste.

I followed all the directions, but my yogurt did not set.

The most common reasons for yogurt not setting are:

- Your yogurt starter may need to be replaced; it may be either old or not contain sufficient live cultures. Get some new starter, add it to the unset batch, and try again.
- The milk temperature was too high when the starter was added and killed the live cultures in the starter. Get some new starter, add it to the unset batch, and try again.

Egg Questions

I followed all the directions, but my eggs are still under-/overcooked or green around the yolks. Why?

Let's just be honest with each other. Eggs are the temperamental fillies of the Instant Pot world. They perform beautifully on a good day, and on other days, they will mess you up. Within the same batch of cooked eggs, the devils with their gray yolks will nestle up innocently beside the angels with their perfect yellow yolks. But with a little experimentation, the pressure cooker can give you perfectly cooked eggs. Since people prefer their eggs at different consistencies, I suggest you experiment to find the time that is best for you.

Recommended cooking times for perfect eggs:

- Soft-boiled: 2 minutes, QPR, ice bath
- Hard-boiled: 5 minutes, 5 minutes NPR, ice bath

Cake Questions

Is the cake really baking in there?

The pressure cooker is not an oven, so the cake is not technically being baked. It is, however, being steamed, resulting in a well-prepared cake.

What is the texture of cakes baked in an Instant Pot?

A cake or quick bread baked in an Instant Pot will be lighter and fluffier than an oven-baked one. Try it for yourself and see how you can make delectable quick breads and cakes without turning on the oven!

Cooking Times

Why does it take so long for the pot to come to pressure?

The amount of time it takes the pot to come to pressure is influenced by:

- The amount of food in the pot. A fuller pot will take longer to come to pressure.
- The type of food in the pot. Liquids take longer to come to pressure than denser foods. Frozen foods will take longer to come to pressure as well.

If I double the ingredients, do I double the cooking time?

No, you keep the cooking time the same. It may take the cooker a little longer to come to pressure, but once under pressure, cooking time is the same. You can vary the number of servings for any of these recipes without increasing the cooking time—under pressure, that is. But the fuller your pot, the longer it will take to come to pressure. Once under pressure, however, one cup of beans will cook as quickly as two cups of beans. So allow longer total cooking times, but do not increase the cooking time under pressure.

Since this question is asked so often, let me use an example. Let's say you're making tea and you need to let the tea steep for 5 minutes. If you're making 4 cups of tea, your 4 cups of water will come to a boil very quickly, and you then steep the tea for 5 minutes. If you're making 10 cups of tea, the 10 cups of water will take longer to come to a boil, but you'll still only steep the tea for 5 minutes. It's the same with pressure cooking. When you double a recipe, the time it takes for the pot to come to pressure increases (boiling 4 cups of water versus 10 cups of water), but the time it takes for the item to cook under pressure stays the same (steeping the tea for 5 minutes).

Can I cook food from frozen without first defrosting it?

Many of these recipes call for frozen vegetables. This is done deliberately. I am using this as a way to slow down cooking so that your vegetables do not overcook.

When should I use natural pressure release versus quick pressure release?

Many of the recipes call for a combination of both. I prefer to use natural release for 10 minutes and then quick release the remaining pressure. There are two situations where I use quick release only:

- Many vegetables require a short cooking time. Natural pressure release results in an overcooked dish, so quick-releasing the pressure is preferable.

- Quick release is often used when you plan to add items to a dish halfway through cooking. This style of cooking in stages can be quite useful in recipes that ask you to cook the beans for a lot longer than the greens. In this case, you release pressure quickly after cooking the beans, add the greens, and then release pressure quickly at the end to avoid overcooking.

LET'S COOK

It's time to start cooking. You know everything you need to know to cook delicious meals in your Instant Pot and to produce food in your own kitchen that will rival what you can get in restaurants. If you can chop, mix, blend, stir, and press buttons, you can make these recipes. None of them call for complicated techniques. Children as young as ten years old have made many of these recipes with success. Children under two years old have eaten these with great enjoyment—as pictures I'm sent of sweet little faces smeared with butternut squash soup often remind me.

Remember that you know your family's tastes better than I do, so if you know they will hate a particular ingredient (hello, cilantro!) or that an ingredient might be too spicy for them (goodbye, cayenne!), change it up to personalize the dish. I am told that I use less salt than many others. Add more or less to suit your tastes.

Finally, keep in mind that when you make these recipes, you'll not only have better-tasting, more authentic, more nutritious food at home, you'll also be saving a lot of money. In just three or four meals, the savings will be enough to justify buying another Instant Pot! If you're looking for a reason to become a two-pot household, now you have it. You're welcome.

Let's use our Instant Pots to explore the varied world of food that awaits us!

VEGETABLES

Creamed Green Beans and Mushrooms

I created this when I was trying to come up with a low-carb version of the traditional green bean casserole. I never cook with canned soups or prepared mixes, and once you taste this easy version, you will see no reason to use canned cream of mushroom soup ever again.

ACTIVE TIME	FUNCTION	RELEASE	TOTAL TIME
10 minutes	Manual (High); Sauté (Normal)	Quick	25 minutes

Egg-Free, Nut-Free, Gluten-Free, Low-Carb • 10 Ingredients or Less • SERVES 8

2 cups finely chopped mushrooms

1 cup chopped onion

3 cloves garlic, minced

1 teaspoon kosher salt

½ teaspoon black pepper

¼ cup water

1 pound trimmed fresh green beans or frozen whole green beans

2 tablespoons diced cream cheese, at room temperature

¼ cup half-and-half

Sliced toasted almonds (optional)

Fried onions (optional)

1. In the Instant Pot, combine the mushrooms, onion, garlic, salt, pepper, and water. Place the green beans on top. Set the cream cheese on top of the beans. Do not stir.

2. Secure the lid on the pot. Close the pressure-release valve. Select MANUAL and set the pot at HIGH pressure for 3 minutes. At the end of the cooking time, use a quick release to depressurize.

3. Select SAUTÉ/NORMAL. Stir in the half-and-half. Cook, stirring frequently, until the sauce has thickened, 1 to 2 minutes. Select CANCEL.

4. Transfer the contents to a serving bowl or platter. Top with almonds and fried onions, if using, and serve.

Coconut Green Beans

Foogath—or veggies with coconut—is a very popular dish in various parts of India, including the western state of Goa. This very simple recipe allows you to taste the green beans but pairs them with naturally nutty and sweet coconut for a wonderful combination.

ACTIVE TIME	FUNCTION	RELEASE	TOTAL TIME
10 minutes	Sauté (Normal); Manual (High)	Quick	25 minutes

Egg-Free, Nut-Free, Dairy-Free, Gluten-Free, Vegan, Low-Carb • 10 Ingredients or Less • SERVES 4

2 tablespoons vegetable oil

1 teaspoon mustard seeds

1 teaspoon cumin seeds

1 cup diced onion

1 teaspoon ground turmeric

1 teaspoon kosher salt

½ teaspoon cayenne pepper

1 (12-ounce) package frozen green beans

¼ cup unsweetened shredded coconut

½ cup water

¼ cup chopped fresh cilantro

1. Select SAUTÉ/NORMAL on the Instant Pot. When the pot is hot, add the oil. Once the oil is hot, add the mustard seeds and cumin seeds, and allow to sizzle for 15 to 20 seconds.

2. Stir in the onion. Add the turmeric, salt, and cayenne and stir to coat. Add the green beans, coconut, and water; stir to combine. Select CANCEL.

3. Secure the lid on the pot. Close the pressure-release valve. Select MANUAL and set the pot at HIGH pressure for 2 minutes. At the end of the cooking time, use a quick release to depressurize.

4. Transfer to a serving dish and garnish with the cilantro. Serve.

Greek-Style Green Beans and Potatoes

I love green beans in the pressure cooker, as every self-respecting Southerner does. In this version, the potatoes and tomatoes make this a very hearty side dish. Serve this with feta cheese and slices of good, crusty, toasted bread on the side, and it can be a main dish. It also goes very well over rice.

ACTIVE TIME	FUNCTION	RELEASE	TOTAL TIME
5 minutes	Manual (High)	Natural + Quick	30 minutes

Egg-Free, Nut-Free, Dairy-Free, Gluten-Free, Vegan • 10 Ingredients or Less • SERVES 6

1 onion, diced

2 cups peeled and cubed (1-inch) russet potatoes

1½ cups diced tomatoes

2 tablespoons olive oil

1 teaspoon granulated sugar (optional)

1 teaspoon kosher salt

½ teaspoon fresh pepper

¼ cup water

4 cups frozen cut green beans or fresh green beans, trimmed and cut into 2-inch pieces

Juice of 1 lemon

¼ cup chopped fresh parsley

1. In the Instant Pot, combine the onion, potatoes, tomatoes, olive oil, sugar (if using), salt, pepper, and water. Stir in the green beans.

2. Secure the lid on the pot. Close the pressure-release valve. Select MANUAL and set the pot at HIGH pressure for 4 minutes. At the end of the cooking time, allow the pot to sit undisturbed for 10 minutes, then quick-release any remaining pressure.

3. Stir in the lemon juice and parsley and serve.

Unstuffed Grape Leaves

Just as in the recipe for Unstuffed Cabbage Rolls (page 75), this is another instance of throwing things into a pot and getting all the same great flavors and textures of the original dish without all of the work. Several folks in my Facebook group say they've tried this with collard greens when they didn't have grape leaves and loved that version as well.

ACTIVE TIME	FUNCTION	RELEASE	TOTAL TIME
15 minutes	Manual (High)	Natural + Quick	40 minutes

Egg-Free, Dairy-Free, Gluten-Free, Vegan • 10 Ingredients or Less • SERVES 4

1 cup chopped onion

1 cup chopped tomato

1 cup basmati rice, rinsed and drained

1 cup pine nuts or slivered almonds

8 ounces brined grape leaves, drained and chopped

2 tablespoons olive oil

3 cloves garlic, minced

1 tablespoon dried parsley or ¼ cup chopped fresh parsley

1½ teaspoons ground allspice

1 teaspoon kosher salt

1 teaspoon black pepper

1 cup water

⅓ cup fresh lemon juice

¼ cup chopped fresh mint

1. In the Instant Pot, combine the onion, tomato, rice, pine nuts, grape leaves, olive oil, garlic, parsley, allspice, salt, pepper, and water. Stir to combine.

2. Secure the lid on the pot. Close the pressure-release valve. Select MANUAL and set the pot at HIGH pressure for 4 minutes. At the end of the cooking time, allow the pot to sit undisturbed for 10 minutes, then quick-release any remaining pressure.

3. Stir in the lemon juice and mint and serve.

Butternut-Ginger Soup

This is one of those dishes that can be made with very few ingredients, yet it tastes like a complex, flavorful, warming soup. Pair it with toasted cheese bread or just have it as a starter.

ACTIVE TIME	FUNCTION	RELEASE	TOTAL TIME
20 minutes	Manual (High)	Natural + Quick	45 minutes

Egg-Free, Nut-Free, Dairy-Free, Gluten-Free, Vegan • 10 Ingredients or Less • SERVES 4 as a side dish; 2 as a main dish

4 cups cubed peeled butternut squash

1 (13.5-ounce) can full-fat coconut milk

1 cup diced onion

3 cloves garlic, minced

1 tablespoon minced fresh ginger

1 teaspoon kosher salt

1 teaspoon black pepper

1 teaspoon ground turmeric

½ teaspoon ground nutmeg, plus more for garnish (optional)

1. In the Instant Pot, combine the squash, coconut milk, onion, garlic, ginger, salt, pepper, turmeric, and the ½ teaspoon nutmeg. Mix well.

2. Secure the lid on the pot. Close the pressure-release valve. Select MANUAL and set the pot at HIGH pressure for 8 minutes. At the end of the cooking time, allow the pot to sit undisturbed for 10 minutes, then quick-release any remaining pressure.

3. Using an immersion blender, purée the soup until smooth. Add a little water, if necessary, to reach desired consistency.

4. Ladle the soup into bowls. Garnish with nutmeg, if desired, and serve.

Garlic-Parmesan Spaghetti Squash

This recipe is all about the flavored oil and the cheese, so don't skimp on either. You can add roasted cherry tomatoes or cranberries for a little pop of color and taste. It calls for just half a squash, but of course you can always use the whole squash and double the other ingredients.

ACTIVE TIME	FUNCTION	RELEASE	TOTAL TIME
20 minutes	Manual (High); Sauté (Normal)	Natural + Quick	45 minutes

Egg-Free, Gluten-Free, Low-Carb • 10 Ingredients or Less • SERVES 4

1 large spaghetti squash

3 tablespoons olive oil

8 cloves garlic, thinly sliced

½ cup slivered almonds

1 teaspoon red pepper flakes

4 cups chopped fresh spinach

1 teaspoon kosher salt

1 cup shredded Parmesan cheese

Variations

Substitute pine nuts or chopped walnuts for almonds.

Add ½ cup dried cranberries to the hot oil along with the garlic, nuts, and red pepper flakes.

Add roasted cherry tomatoes to the finished dish.

Substitute crumbled feta cheese for the shredded Parmesan.

Add ¼ cup chopped fresh basil along with the spaghetti squash.

1. Using the tip of a sharp, short knife, pierce the squash in 7 to 8 places.

2. Pour 1½ cups water into the Instant Pot. Place a trivet in the pot. Set the squash on the trivet.

3. Secure the lid on the pot. Close the pressure-release valve. Select MANUAL and set the pot at HIGH pressure for 7 minutes. At the end of the cooking time, allow the pot to sit undisturbed for 10 minutes, then quick-release any remaining pressure.

4. Remove the squash, and cut it in half lengthwise. Store one half in a tightly sealed container in the refrigerator for another use. Without destroying the shell, use a fork to scrape the strands of the remaining half into a large bowl. Measure out 4 cups (save any remaining squash for another use). Set the squash shell aside to use as a serving vessel. Empty the pot and wipe dry.

5. Select SAUTÉ/NORMAL. When the pot is hot, add the olive oil. Once the oil is hot, add the garlic, almonds, and pepper flakes. Cook, stirring constantly and being careful not to burn the garlic, for about 1 minute. Add the spinach, salt, and spaghetti squash. Stir well to thoroughly combine ingredients until the spinach wilts.

6. Transfer the mixture to the reserved squash shell. Sprinkle with the Parmesan cheese just before serving.

Vegetable Curry with Tofu

I don't often use prepared spice mixes, but the effort involved in making Japanese curry paste cubes at home is not practical for weeknight dinners. This is one of those mild curries that everyone can enjoy—even if the curry cubes say "hot," they're not really hot, just flavorful.

ACTIVE TIME	FUNCTION	RELEASE	TOTAL TIME
10 minutes	Manual (High)	Natural + Quick	35 minutes

Egg-Free, Nut-Free, Dairy-Free, Vegan • 10 Ingredients or Less • SERVES 4

2 cups diced peeled butternut squash

2 cups chopped bok choy

1 cup stemmed, seeded, and roughly chopped yellow bell pepper

1 cup button or cremini mushrooms, trimmed and quartered

1 block Japanese curry paste, diced

2 cups water

1 (14-ounce) package firm tofu, diced

Rice (optional)

1. In the Instant Pot, combine the squash, bok choy, bell pepper, mushrooms, curry paste, and water. Stir well.

2. Secure the lid on the pot. Close the pressure-release valve. Select MANUAL and set the pot at HIGH pressure for 4 minutes. At the end of the cooking time, allow the pot to sit undisturbed for 10 minutes, then quick-release any remaining pressure.

3. Open the lid and stir. Very gently stir in the tofu.

4. Serve the curry with rice, if desired.

Tex-Mex Corn Pudding

While I typically love this with a hearty side of bean stew, I often just top it with a little extra-spicy pico de gallo and eat just that as a snack.

ACTIVE TIME	FUNCTION	RELEASE	TOTAL TIME
5 minutes	Manual (High)	Natural	50 minutes

Nut-Free • 10 Ingredients or Less • SERVES 8

Vegetable oil

1 (8-ounce) package corn bread mix

1 (14-ounce) can creamed corn

1 (4.5-ounce) can chopped mild green chiles

½ cup whole milk

2 large eggs, lightly beaten

¼ cup water

Pico de gallo, for garnish (optional)

1. Grease a 6×3-inch round springform pan with vegetable oil; set aside.

2. In a large bowl, combine the corn bread mix, creamed corn, chiles, milk, eggs, and water. Mix well. Transfer the corn mixture to the pan; cover with foil.

3. Pour 2 cups water into the Instant Pot. Place a trivet in the pot. Place the pan on the trivet.

4. Secure the lid on the pot. Close the pressure-release valve. Select MANUAL and set the pot at HIGH pressure for 25 minutes. At the end of the cooking time, use a natural release to depressurize.

5. Let the pudding cool to room temperature, and then run a knife along the edges to separate the pudding from the sides of the pan. Carefully unclasp the springform ring and remove it. Garnish with pico de gallo, if desired, and serve.

NOTE: Some brands of corn bread and muffin mix contain animal shortening (lard). Read the label to be sure the mix you buy is vegetarian.

Cajun Corn Chowder (page 52)

Cajun Corn Chowder

Traditional *maque choux* is a dry side dish, but I think it lends itself very well to a chunky, thick, creamy, spicy chowder. I often use a package or two of frozen mirepoix to save time chopping the veggies.

ACTIVE TIME	FUNCTION	RELEASE	TOTAL TIME
15 minutes	Manual (High)	Natural + Quick	40 minutes

Egg-Free, Nut-Free, Dairy-Free, Gluten-Free • 10 Ingredients or Less • SERVES 6

1 (10-ounce) package frozen corn

2 cups quartered baby potatoes

1 cup canned diced tomatoes, undrained

1 cup diced onion

1 cup stemmed, seeded, and diced green bell pepper

1 cup diced celery

2 teaspoons Cajun seasoning

1 teaspoon kosher salt

1 cup water

½ cup heavy cream, half-and-half, or almond milk

¼ cup chopped fresh thyme

1. In the Instant Pot, combine the corn, potatoes, tomatoes, onion, bell pepper, celery, Cajun seasoning, salt, and water. Mix well.

2. Secure the lid on the pot. Close the pressure-release valve. Select MANUAL and set the pot at HIGH pressure for 5 minutes. At the end of the cooking time, allow the pot to sit undisturbed for 10 minutes, then quick-release any remaining pressure. Stir in the cream.

3. Using an immersion blender, purée some of the soup to thicken slightly. Add a little water, if necessary, to reach the desired consistency.

4. Stir in the thyme and serve.

Butter "Chicken" with Soy Curls

This recipe is based on my famous butter chicken, and I assure you it does not lack for taste or wonderful texture. I have used very little soy or manufactured protein in this book, but in this case, it's well worth the exception.

ACTIVE TIME	FUNCTION	RELEASE	TOTAL TIME
15 minutes	Manual (High); Sauté (Normal)	Natural + Quick	40 minutes

Egg-Free, Nut-Free, Dairy-Free, Gluten-Free, Vegan, Low-Carb • SERVES 4

1 (14.5-ounce) can diced tomatoes

1½ cups dry Soy Curls

5 to 6 cloves garlic, minced

1 to 2 teaspoons minced fresh ginger

1 teaspoon ground turmeric

½ teaspoon cayenne pepper

1 teaspoon smoked paprika

1 teaspoon kosher salt

2 teaspoons garam masala

1 teaspoon ground cumin

1 cup water

½ cup (1 stick) cold butter, cut into cubes, or coconut oil

½ cup heavy cream or full-fat coconut milk

¼ to ½ cup chopped fresh cilantro

Hot cooked basmati rice, naan, or riced cauliflower, for serving

1. In the Instant Pot, combine the tomatoes, Soy Curls, garlic, ginger, turmeric, cayenne, paprika, salt, 1 teaspoon of the garam masala, cumin, and water.

2. Secure the lid on the pot. Close the pressure-release valve. Select MANUAL and set the pot at HIGH pressure for 6 minutes. At the end of the cooking time, allow the pot to sit undisturbed for 10 minutes, then quick-release any remaining pressure.

3. Select SAUTÉ/NORMAL. When the pot is hot, add the butter and cream. Stir gently until the butter is melted. Use the back of your spoon to crush any large tomato pieces. Select CANCEL.

4. Stir in the remaining 1 teaspoon of the garam masala and the cilantro.

5. Serve with rice, naan, or riced cauliflower.

Butter "Chicken" with Soy Curls (page 53)

Jamaican Mixed Vegetable Curry

This dish is one of the few times I think it's okay to use a prepared curry powder! You can mix and match different vegetables for this dish—just ensure that they all cook approximately the same time. Pair this with Coconut Red Beans and Rice (page 174) and you'll have a lovely dinner.

ACTIVE TIME	FUNCTION	RELEASE	TOTAL TIME
25 minutes	Sauté (Normal); Manual (High)	Natural + Quick	50 minutes

Egg-Free, Nut-Free, Dairy-Free, Gluten-Free, Vegan • 10 Ingredients or Less • SERVES 6

2 tablespoons vegetable oil

3 cloves garlic, minced

1 tablespoon minced fresh ginger

1 cup chopped onion

1 tablespoon plus 1½ teaspoons Jamaican curry powder

1 stemmed, seeded, and sliced Scotch bonnet pepper

3 sprigs fresh thyme or ½ teaspoon dried thyme

1 teaspoon kosher salt

½ teaspoon ground allspice

4 cups (1-inch cubes) peeled pumpkin

1½ cups (1-inch cubes) peeled potatoes

2 cups stemmed, seeded, and diced red, yellow, or orange bell peppers

1 cup water

Cooked rice, for serving

1. Select SAUTÉ/NORMAL on the Instant Pot. When the pot is hot, add the vegetable oil. Once the oil is hot, add the garlic and ginger. Cook, stirring, for 20 seconds.

2. Stir in the onion and cook, 1 to 2 minutes. Add the curry powder, Scotch bonnet pepper, thyme, salt, and allspice. Stir well to coat. (At this point, if you have any browning or sticking at the bottom of the pot, use ¼ to ⅓ cup water to deglaze the pot, scraping up the browned bits and allowing the water to evaporate.)

3. Add the pumpkin, potatoes, bell peppers, and water. Select CANCEL.

4. Secure the lid on the pot. Close the pressure-release valve. Select MANUAL and set the pot at HIGH pressure for 3 minutes. At the end of the cooking time, allow the pot to sit undisturbed for 10 minutes, then quick-release any remaining pressure.

5. Open the lid and use the back of a spoon to mash some of the vegetables to thicken the curry, if desired.

6. Ladle the curry into individual bowls over rice and serve.

Beet and Lentil Salad (page 60)

Beet and Lentil Salad

I had this salad at an airport restaurant, if you can believe it. I've spent much of my life so far in airports and airplanes, so I suppose I was bound to run into good food. I've long since forgotten which airport and which client, but I haven't forgotten this salad. If you can get beets with fresh-looking leaves still attached, wash the leaves and cut them into ribbons or large pieces, and serve your salad on the beet greens. Top with feta cheese for additional bite, or eat as is. This salad just keeps getting better as it marinates in the fridge, so make extra. It's just as good cold as it is warm.

ACTIVE TIME	FUNCTION	RELEASE	TOTAL TIME
10 minutes	Manual (High)	Natural + Quick	40 minutes

Egg-Free, Nut-Free, Dairy-Free, Gluten-Free, Vegan • 10 Ingredients or Less • SERVES 4

For the Salad

1 cup French lentils

1 teaspoon kosher salt

1¼ cups water

2 large red or golden beets, scrubbed, trimmed, and quartered

For the Dressing

½ cup red wine vinegar

¼ cup olive oil

1 tablespoon Dijon mustard

2 teaspoons chopped fresh oregano

1 teaspoon kosher salt

½ teaspoon cayenne pepper

Beet greens, cut into ribbons or left whole (optional)

1. **For the salad:** In the Instant Pot, combine the lentils, salt, and water.

2. Place a trivet on top of the lentils. Place the beets on the trivet.

3. Secure the lid on the pot. Close the pressure-release valve. Select MANUAL and set the pot at HIGH pressure for 10 minutes. At the end of the cooking time, allow the pot to sit undisturbed for 10 minutes, then quick-release any remaining pressure.

4. Remove the beets, and once cooled, peel and dice. Mix the beets with the lentils in a large serving bowl or on a platter.

5. **For the dressing:** In a small bowl, whisk together the vinegar, oil, mustard, oregano, salt, and cayenne. Pour the dressing over the beets and lentils. Toss to coat.

6. Serve the salad over the beet greens, if desired.

NOTE: French lentils—also called green or du Puy lentils—are smaller than brown lentils. They hold their shape better than brown lentils after cooking and have a lightly peppery flavor.

Creamy Beet-Yogurt Dip with Dill and Garlic

I love making beets in the pressure cooker. They cook quickly, they don't stain your whole kitchen, and when made up into this beautiful dip inspired by *borani*—a Persian dip that combines cooked vegetables with thick yogurt—they grace your table with a little splash of color.

ACTIVE TIME	FUNCTION	RELEASE	TOTAL TIME
10 minutes	Manual (High)	Natural + Quick	40 minutes

Egg-Free, Nut-Free • 10 Ingredients or Less • SERVES 4

2 large red or golden beets, scrubbed, trimmed, and quartered

1 cup Greek yogurt

3 cloves garlic, minced

2 tablespoons fresh lemon juice

1 teaspoon kosher salt

¼ cup chopped fresh dill

2 tablespoons black or white sesame seeds (optional)

Lavash, pita triangles, and/or crudités, for serving

1. Pour 1½ cups water into the Instant Pot. Place a trivet in the pot. Set the beets on the trivet.

2. Secure the lid on the pot. Close the pressure-release valve. Select MANUAL and set the pot at HIGH pressure for 10 minutes. At the end of the cooking time, allow the pot to sit undisturbed for 10 minutes, then quick-release any remaining pressure.

3. Allow the beets to cool, or run them under cold water; peel. (The peel should slide right off.)

4. In a blender or food processor, combine the beets, yogurt, garlic, lemon juice, and salt. Blend or process until smooth.

5. Transfer the dip to a bowl. Sprinkle with dill and sesame seeds, if desired.

6. Serve with lavash, pita triangles, and/or crudités.

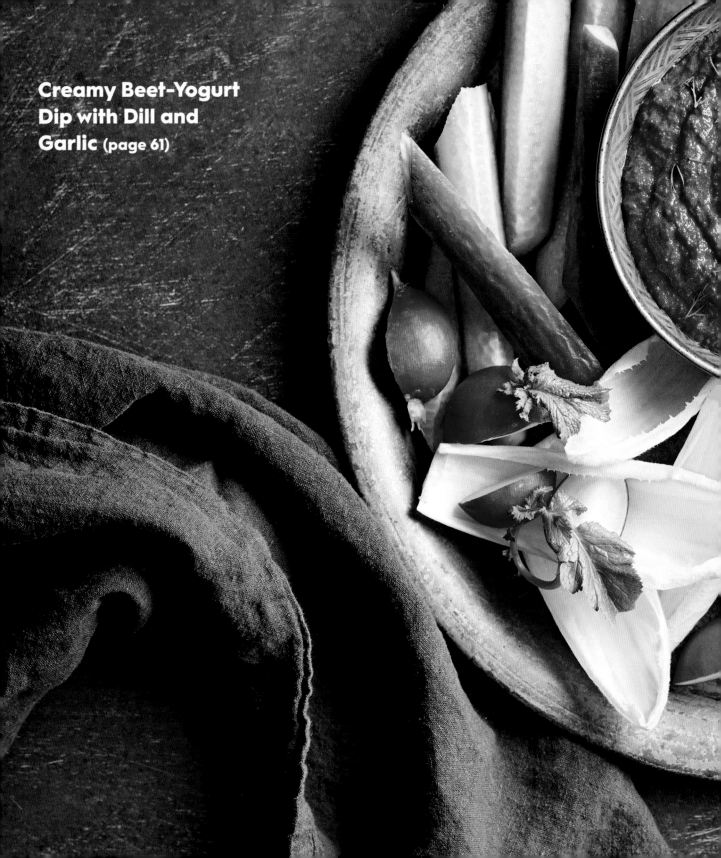

Creamy Beet-Yogurt Dip with Dill and Garlic (page 61)

Minty Peas

This is just a burst of spring in your mouth—an elegant, colorful, fast, and fresh side dish to liven up dinner. If you've never used a 0 minutes setting, think of it just as you would setting your pot for 1 minute—but you're using 0 minutes. The pot will come to pressure, and as soon as it does, it will turn itself off. Then, you'll release all remaining pressure, and you'll have perfectly cooked, tender peas with crisp-tender onions and peppers.

ACTIVE TIME	FUNCTION	RELEASE	TOTAL TIME
10 minutes	Manual (High)	Quick	20 minutes

Egg-Free, Nut-Free, Dairy-Free, Gluten-Free, Vegan • 10 Ingredients or Less • SERVES 4

2 cups frozen peas

1 cup thinly sliced onion

1 cup stemmed, seeded, and diced red bell pepper

2 tablespoons water or vegetable broth

1 tablespoon butter, melted, or olive oil

1 teaspoon kosher salt

½ teaspoon black pepper

2 tablespoons chopped fresh mint

Zest of 1 lemon

1 tablespoon fresh lemon juice

1. In the Instant Pot, combine the peas, onion, bell pepper, water, butter, salt, and pepper. Stir to combine.

2. Secure the lid on the pot. Close the pressure-release valve. Select MANUAL and set the pot at HIGH pressure for 0 minutes. At the end of the cooking time, use a quick release to depressurize.

3. Stir in the mint and the lemon zest and juice and serve.

Summer Squash Couscous

The combination of Israeli couscous with vegetables makes this a good two-in-one side dish. I like to eat some hot the first day, and then use leftovers in a salad the next day.

ACTIVE TIME	FUNCTION	RELEASE	TOTAL TIME
15 minutes	Manual (High)	Natural + Quick	30 minutes

Egg-Free, Nut-Free, Dairy-Free, Vegan · SERVES 6

½ cup diced onion

3 cloves garlic, minced

2 cups diced tomatoes (2 large)

2 cups (1-inch cubes) zucchini (1 large)

1 cup (1-inch cubes) yellow squash (1 small)

1 cup Israeli couscous

1 teaspoon kosher salt

½ teaspoon ground turmeric

1 teaspoon ground cumin

½ teaspoon ground cinnamon

½ teaspoon ground allspice

1 cup water

Juice of 1 large lime

¼ cup chopped fresh parsley (optional)

1. In the Instant Pot, combine the onion, garlic, tomatoes, zucchini, yellow squash, couscous, salt, turmeric, cumin, cinnamon, allspice, and water.

2. Secure the lid on the pot. Close the pressure-release valve. Select MANUAL and set the pot at HIGH pressure for 3 minutes. At the end of the cooking time, allow the pot to sit undisturbed for 5 minutes, then quick-release any remaining pressure.

3. Stir to fluff up the couscous.

4. Mix in the lime juice and parsley, if using, and serve.

Sweet-and-Spicy Glazed Brussels Sprouts

I know a lot of people only like their Brussels sprouts browned and crisp, but if you like steamed Brussels sprouts, you will love this. You will love the sauce on anything, by the way, so you may want to try the sauce with steamed broccoli or cauliflower if Brussels sprouts aren't your thing.

ACTIVE TIME	FUNCTION	RELEASE	TOTAL TIME
15 minutes	Manual (High)	Quick	30 minutes

Egg-Free, Nut-Free, Dairy-Free, Gluten-Free, Vegan • 10 Ingredients or Less • SERVES 6

2 pounds small Brussels sprouts, rinsed and trimmed

1 cup dried cranberries

½ cup orange marmalade

2 tablespoons butter or vegan butter substitute, melted

1 teaspoon kosher salt

½ to 1 teaspoon cayenne pepper

Chopped toasted walnuts (optional)

1. Pour 1½ cups water into the Instant Pot. Place a steamer basket in the pot. Place the Brussels sprouts and cranberries in the steamer basket.

2. Secure the lid on the pot. Close the pressure-release valve. Select MANUAL and set the pot at HIGH pressure for 3 minutes. At the end of the cooking time, use a quick release to depressurize.

3. Transfer the Brussels sprouts and cranberries to a serving bowl. Add the marmalade, butter, salt, cayenne, and walnuts, if using. Toss well to combine. Serve hot.

Braised Cabbage Pasta

I used *haluski*—a traditional Polish dish of egg noodles, fried cabbage, and onion—as the inspiration for this dish. Some versions include sausage, but I find this vegetarian version to be very comforting and filling.

ACTIVE TIME	FUNCTION	RELEASE	TOTAL TIME
15 minutes	Manual (High)	Natural + Quick	40 minutes

Egg-Free, Nut-Free, Dairy-Free, Vegan • 10 Ingredients or Less • SERVES 4

4 cups chopped green cabbage

1 cup sliced button or cremini mushrooms

1 cup diced onion

2 tablespoons butter or vegan butter substitute, melted

1 teaspoon ground marjoram

1 teaspoon kosher salt

1 teaspoon black pepper

2 cups dried bow-tie pasta

1½ cups water

1 cup frozen peas and carrots

1. In the Instant Pot, combine the cabbage, mushrooms, onion, butter, marjoram, salt, and pepper. Add the pasta and water; mix well.

2. Scatter the peas and carrots on top of the mixture. Do not stir.

3. Secure the lid on the pot. Close the pressure-release valve. Select MANUAL and set the pot at HIGH pressure for 5 minutes. At the end of the cooking time, allow the pot to sit undisturbed for 10 minutes, then quick-release any remaining pressure.

4. Spoon into individual bowls and serve.

Variations

Replace 2 cups of the chopped cabbage with 2 cups sauerkraut for a tangier version.

Turmeric-Spiced Cabbage and Potatoes

This vibrant-colored dish is easy and approachable, and it has wide appeal. It's very mildly spiced, making it perfect for the whole family. I like to serve it with an Indian naan because a little fusion cooking never hurt anyone.

ACTIVE TIME	FUNCTION	RELEASE	TOTAL TIME
15 minutes	Manual (High)	Quick	30 minutes

Egg-Free, Nut-Free, Dairy-Free, Gluten-Free, Vegan • 10 Ingredients or Less • SERVES 6

2 tablespoons vegetable oil

1 teaspoon ground turmeric

1 teaspoon kosher salt

1 teaspoon smoked paprika

1 teaspoon ground cumin

¼ cup water

2 cups peeled and chopped (1-inch pieces) russet potatoes

3 medium carrots, peeled and cut into 2-inch pieces

1 cup chopped onion

3 cups coarsely chopped cabbage

Cooked rice, naan, flatbread, or injera, for serving

1. In the Instant Pot, combine the oil, turmeric, salt, paprika, cumin, and water. Stir well.

2. Add the potatoes, carrots, and onion; stir to combine. Add the cabbage on top. Do not stir.

3. Secure the lid on the pot. Close the pressure-release valve. Select MANUAL and set the pot at HIGH pressure for 2 minutes. At the end of the cooking time, use a quick release to depressurize.

4. Serve with rice, naan, flatbread, or injera.

Sweet-and-Sour Red Cabbage

Sweet, sour, tangy, hearty—such a great combination of tastes and so pretty to look at as well! I don't know why I don't make this all the time. The leftovers taste great as well.

ACTIVE TIME	FUNCTION	RELEASE	TOTAL TIME
15 minutes	Manual (High)	Quick	30 minutes

Egg-Free, Nut-Free, Dairy-Free, Gluten-Free, Vegan • 10 Ingredients or Less • SERVES 4

6 cups chopped red cabbage

3 small Granny Smith apples, unpeeled, cored, and cut into 1-inch wedges

⅓ cup apple cider vinegar, plus more if desired

2 to 3 tablespoons granulated sugar

2 tablespoons butter, melted, or vegetable oil

1 teaspoon kosher salt

½ teaspoon black pepper

¼ teaspoon ground cloves

2 bay leaves

1. In the Instant Pot, combine the cabbage, apples, vinegar, sugar, butter, salt, pepper, cloves, and bay leaves. Stir to combine.

2. Secure the lid on the pot. Close the pressure-release valve. Select MANUAL and set the pot at HIGH pressure for 3 minutes. At the end of the cooking time, use a quick release to depressurize.

3. Taste and add a little more vinegar, if needed.

4. Remove the bay leaves before serving.

Unstuffed Cabbage Rolls

I am a lazy foodie, as many of you know. If it's possible to skip a step but still get good taste—I'm skipping it. I'm skipping rolling the cabbage in this recipe, and no one will care. It's got all the traditional flavor of cabbage rolls but it comes together in less than half the time.

ACTIVE TIME	FUNCTION	RELEASE	TOTAL TIME
10 minutes	Manual (High)	Natural + Quick	35 minutes

Egg-Free, Nut-Free, Dairy-Free, Vegan • 10 Ingredients or Less • SERVES 4

6 cups chopped green cabbage

2 medium onions, chopped

1 (14.5-ounce) can diced tomatoes

1 (8-ounce) can tomato sauce

1 cup fine bulgur

3 cloves garlic, minced

2 teaspoons kosher salt

1 teaspoon black pepper

1 teaspoon granulated sugar

¼ cup water

2 tablespoons apple cider vinegar

1. In the Instant Pot, combine the cabbage, onion, tomatoes, tomato sauce, bulgur, garlic, salt, pepper, sugar, and water. Stir well to combine.

2. Secure the lid on the pot. Close the pressure-release valve. Select MANUAL and set the pot at HIGH pressure for 3 minutes. At the end of the cooking time, allow the pot to sit undisturbed for 10 minutes, then quick-release any remaining pressure.

3. Stir in the vinegar and serve.

NOTE: Bulgur comes in different grinds—coarse, medium, and fine. Medium grind is the most common, but you'll want to seek out the fine grind for this recipe—which is also most often recommended for tabbouleh.

Smoky Braised Kale with Tomatoes

Inspired by a Kenyan greens recipe, this simple but flavorful dish of greens and tomatoes is smoky and much more flavorful than the list of ingredients would suggest. Sometimes when I'm craving something spicy, I chop up a few serrano peppers to add to it, and just eat the greens and rice for dinner.

ACTIVE TIME	FUNCTION	RELEASE	TOTAL TIME
10 minutes	Manual (High)	Natural + Quick	35 minutes

Egg-Free, Nut-Free, Dairy-Free, Gluten-Free, Vegan, Low-Carb • 10 Ingredients or Less • SERVES 4

2 cups diced tomatoes

1 cup chopped onion

3 cloves garlic, minced

2 teaspoons smoked paprika

1 teaspoon ground turmeric

½ teaspoon ground coriander

1 cube vegetable bouillon, crushed (optional)

½ cup water

6 cups chopped kale

Juice of 1 lemon

1. In the Instant Pot, combine the tomatoes, onion, garlic, paprika, turmeric, coriander, bouillon, and water. Stir to combine. Stir in the kale.

2. Secure the lid on the pot. Close the pressure-release valve. Select MANUAL and set the pot at HIGH pressure for 5 minutes. At the end of the cooking time, allow the pot to sit undisturbed for 10 minutes, then quick-release any remaining pressure.

3. Stir in the lemon juice and serve.

Tangy Okra and Tomatoes

Okay, I know some of you are wondering about whether or not this is an...umm...there's no polite way to say this...a slimy okra dish. It is not! Would I give you a recipe for a slimy dish? I most decidedly would not. Leaving the okra whole, using vinegar, and cooking for a bit longer keep this dish fresh and appetizing.

ACTIVE TIME	FUNCTION	RELEASE	TOTAL TIME
10 minutes	Manual (High)	Natural + Quick	25 minutes

Egg-Free, Nut-Free, Dairy-Free, Gluten-Free, Vegan, Low-Carb · 10 Ingredients or Less · SERVES 4

1 (14.5-ounce) can diced tomatoes

2 tablespoons apple cider vinegar

1 cup diced onion

3 cloves garlic, minced

2 vegetable bouillon cubes, crushed

1 teaspoon smoked paprika

1 teaspoon kosher salt

¼ to ½ teaspoon ground allspice

½ cup water

1½ pounds okra, fresh or frozen

2 tablespoons tomato paste

1 tablespoon fresh lemon juice

1. In the Instant Pot, combine the tomatoes, vinegar, onion, garlic, bouillon cubes, paprika, salt, allspice, and ¼ cup of the water. Place the okra on top of the tomato mixture.

2. Secure the lid on the pot. Close the pressure-release valve. Select MANUAL and set the pot at HIGH pressure for 2 minutes. At the end of the cooking time, allow the pot to sit undisturbed for 5 minutes, then quick-release any remaining pressure.

3. In a small bowl, stir the tomato paste into the remaining ¼ cup water to dissolve.

4. Gently stir the tomato paste mixture into the pot along with the lemon juice, and serve.

Kimchi Stew

On a cold night, there's nothing more comforting than a hearty, spicy soup. Using prepared kimchi packs a huge punch of flavor with very little effort.

ACTIVE TIME	FUNCTION	RELEASE	TOTAL TIME
10 minutes	Manual (High)	Natural + Quick	30 minutes

Egg-Free, Nut-Free, Dairy-Free, Vegan, Low-Carb • SERVES 4

2 cups kimchi

1 cup chopped onion

1 cup dried shiitake mushrooms

3 cloves garlic, minced

1 tablespoon minced fresh ginger

1 tablespoon toasted sesame oil

1 tablespoon dark soy sauce

1 tablespoon gochugaru (Korean ground red pepper) or ½ teaspoon cayenne pepper

½ teaspoon granulated sugar

½ teaspoon kosher salt

2 cups water

½ cup chopped green onions

1 (8-ounce) package firm tofu, diced

1. In the Instant Pot, combine the kimchi, onion, mushrooms, garlic, ginger, sesame oil, soy sauce, gochugaru, sugar, salt, and water.

2. Secure the lid on the pot. Close the pressure-release valve. Select MANUAL and set the pot at HIGH pressure for 3 minutes. At the end of the cooking time, allow the pot to sit undisturbed for 10 minutes, then quick-release any remaining pressure.

3. Stir in the green onions and tofu and serve.

NOTE: Dark soy sauce—also called Chinese black soy sauce—is a dark brown and slightly thick soy sauce. It is less salty than regular soy sauce and has a lightly sweet flavor.

Summer Vegetable Soup

This soup is so pretty and light—yet filling. Stirring in the raw garlic and parsley at the end and topping it with the Parmesan are the keys to getting a good combination of flavorful broth and vegetables, but also lending a fresh taste to this soup.

ACTIVE TIME	FUNCTION	RELEASE	TOTAL TIME
15 minutes	Manual (High); Sauté (Normal)	Quick	30 minutes

Egg-Free, Nut-Free, Gluten-Free, Low-Carb • 10 Ingredients or Less • SERVES 6

8 cups chopped rainbow chard

4 cups thinly sliced leeks (white and light green parts)

2 cups vegetable broth, plus more if needed

1 (14.5-ounce) can chickpeas, drained and rinsed

1 cup sliced celery

6 cloves garlic, minced

1 teaspoon dried oregano

1 teaspoon kosher salt

2 teaspoons black pepper

1 medium yellow summer squash, halved lengthwise and sliced

¼ cup chopped fresh parsley

4 to 6 tablespoons grated Parmesan cheese

1. In the Instant Pot, combine the chard, leeks, broth, chickpeas, celery, half the garlic, the oregano, salt, and pepper.

2. Secure the lid on the pot. Close the pressure-release valve. Select MANUAL and set the pot at HIGH pressure for 3 minutes. At the end of the cooking time, use a quick release to depressurize. Add more broth, if needed.

3. Select SAUTÉ/NORMAL. Add the squash, parsley, and remaining garlic and cook, stirring occasionally, 2 to 3 minutes.

4. Ladle the soup into bowls, sprinkle with the Parmesan cheese, and serve.

NOTE: To make this dish vegan, omit the Parmesan cheese.

Hearty Greens and Potato Stew

Collard greens or kale combine with potatoes to make a simple but filling vegetable stew. Add a grilled cheese sandwich on the side, and you've got yourself a great meal.

ACTIVE TIME	FUNCTION	RELEASE	TOTAL TIME
15 minutes	Manual (High)	Natural + Quick	40 minutes

Egg-Free, Nut-Free, Dairy-Free, Gluten-Free, Vegan • 10 Ingredients or Less • SERVES 8

4 cups coarsely chopped collard greens or kale

4 cups vegetable broth or water

2 cups peeled and cubed (2-inch) potatoes

1 cup diced onion

1 cup diced tomato

1 tablespoon plus ¼ cup extra-virgin olive oil

3 cloves garlic, minced

2 teaspoons kosher salt

1 teaspoon black pepper

¼ cup red wine vinegar

1. In the Instant Pot, combine the collard greens, broth, potatoes, onion, tomato, 1 tablespoon of the olive oil, garlic, salt, and pepper.

2. Secure the lid on the pot. Close the pressure-release valve. Select MANUAL and set the pot at HIGH pressure for 4 minutes. At the end of the cooking time, allow the pot to sit undisturbed for 10 minutes, then quick-release any remaining pressure.

3. Add the vinegar. Using an immersion blender, blend the soup until thick and chunky, but not entirely puréed.

4. Warm the remaining ¼ cup of the olive oil in a small saucepan over medium heat.

5. Divide the soup among 8 serving bowls. Drizzle each serving with a generous teaspoon of the warm oil and serve.

Eggplant-Tomato Stew with Chickpeas and Fresh Basil (page 86)

Eggplant-Tomato Stew with Chickpeas and Fresh Basil

I was surprised when I realized that many people had never cooked eggplant at home. So now, I love hiding eggplant in various dishes. The combination of flavors in this stew makes it a light but satisfying dish. Add some good-quality fragrant olive oil to the top of the hot soup before serving for a last-minute burst of flavor.

ACTIVE TIME	FUNCTION	RELEASE	TOTAL TIME
15 minutes	Sauté (Normal); Manual (High)	Natural + Quick	35 minutes

Egg-Free, Nut-Free, Dairy-Free, Gluten-Free, Vegan, Low-Carb • 10 Ingredients or Less • SERVES 4

3 tablespoons vegetable oil

3 cloves garlic, minced

4 cups peeled, chopped eggplant

1 (14.5-ounce) can chickpeas, drained and rinsed

2 cups chopped tomatoes or 1 (14.5-ounce) can diced tomatoes

1 cup chopped onion

1 cup stemmed, seeded, and roughly chopped red, yellow, or orange bell pepper

1 teaspoon kosher salt

1 teaspoon black pepper

¼ cup chopped fresh basil

Extra-virgin olive oil, for serving (optional)

1. Select SAUTÉ/NORMAL on the Instant Pot. When the pot is hot, add the vegetable oil. Once the oil is hot, add the garlic and allow it to sizzle for about 30 seconds. Select CANCEL.

2. Add the eggplant, chickpeas, if using, tomatoes, onion, bell pepper, salt, and pepper.

3. Secure the lid on the pot. Close the pressure-release valve. Select MANUAL and set the pot at HIGH pressure for 4 minutes. At the end of the cooking time, allow the pot to sit undisturbed for 5 minutes, then quick-release any remaining pressure.

4. Ladle the stew into bowls and garnish with the basil. Drizzle with olive oil, if desired, and serve.

Coconut-Cabbage Soup

This is not like any other Thai curry you've had. It's a Thai-like soup. All a soup needs to be is delicious and filling, and I think this thick, stewlike soup accomplishes both. You could also add some reconstituted rice noodles after it's done cooking, or just eat it over hot cooked rice.

ACTIVE TIME	FUNCTION	RELEASE	TOTAL TIME
10 minutes	Manual (High)	Quick	20 minutes

Egg-Free, Nut-Free, Dairy-Free, Gluten-Free, Vegan, Low-Carb • SERVES 6

2 tablespoons green or yellow curry paste

2 tablespoons gluten-free soy sauce

1 tablespoon granulated sugar

½ teaspoon kosher salt

1 (13.5-ounce) can full-fat coconut milk

3 cups water

4 cups thickly sliced green cabbage

1 (15-ounce) can straw mushrooms, drained

½ cup chopped fresh cilantro

1 cup cherry tomatoes

1 cup stemmed, seeded, and diced red bell pepper

Zest of 1 lime

2 tablespoons fresh lime juice

1. In the Instant Pot, combine the curry paste, soy sauce, sugar, and salt. Mix well. Add half the coconut milk and the water, stirring to dissolve the curry paste. Set aside the remaining coconut milk.

2. Stir in the cabbage, mushrooms, and cilantro. Scatter the tomatoes and bell pepper over the top. Do not stir.

3. Secure the lid on the pot. Close the pressure-release valve. Select MANUAL and set the pot at HIGH pressure for 0 minutes. At the end of the cooking time, use a quick release to depressurize.

4. Stir in the remaining coconut milk and the lime zest and juice and serve.

Coconut–Cabbage Soup (page 87)

Tortellini Soup with Kale

Perfect for those nights when you just can't figure out what you're having, this throw-together soup is hearty, filling, and family-friendly. Add some toasted bread and a few slices of cheese, and dinner is served.

ACTIVE TIME	FUNCTION	RELEASE	TOTAL TIME
10 minutes	Manual (High)	Natural + Quick	30 minutes

Egg-Free, Nut-Free • 10 Ingredients or Less • SERVES 4

1 cup chopped onion

3 cloves garlic, minced

2 teaspoons Italian seasoning

1 cup diced canned or fresh tomatoes

3 tablespoons tomato paste

1 teaspoon kosher salt

5 cups water

1 (9-ounce) package fresh cheese tortellini

8 ounces chopped kale, fresh or frozen

Grated Parmesan cheese, for garnish (optional)

Chopped fresh basil, for garnish (optional)

1. In the Instant Pot, combine the onion, garlic, Italian seasoning, tomatoes, tomato paste, salt, water, tortellini, and kale. Stir well to combine.

2. Secure the lid on the pot. Close the pressure-release valve. Select MANUAL and set the pot at HIGH pressure for 3 minutes. At the end of the cooking time, allow the pot to sit undisturbed for 5 minutes, then quick-release any remaining pressure.

3. Ladle into bowls and top with Parmesan cheese and basil, if using. Serve.

Sicilian Sweet-and-
Sour Eggplant (page 94)

Sicilian Sweet-and-Sour Eggplant

Sweet, hot, tangy, and spicy, this caponata is such a burst of flavors in your mouth. No eggplant taste, just the taste of deliciousness. Don't skip the sautéing step—you want a thick, syrupy mixture, and the extra 3 to 5 minutes at the end are totally worth it. Serve this over toasted bread—as in crostini or bruschetta—as a delicious dip or side dish.

ACTIVE TIME	FUNCTION	RELEASE	TOTAL TIME
20 minutes	Manual (High); Sauté (Normal)	Natural + Quick	35 minutes

Egg-Free, Nut-Free, Dairy-Free, Gluten-Free, Vegan, Low-Carb • 10 Ingredients or Less • SERVES 6

4 cups (1-inch cubes) peeled eggplant (1 medium)

1 cup chopped tomato

1 cup chopped onion

3 cloves garlic, minced

2 tablespoons tomato paste

2 tablespoons granulated sugar

2 tablespoons olive oil

¼ cup water

2 tablespoons balsamic vinegar

1 teaspoon kosher salt

½ teaspoon coarsely ground black pepper

¼ cup capers

¼ cup sliced green olives

¼ cup chopped fresh parsley

¼ cup pine nuts or chopped walnuts, toasted (optional)

1. In the Instant Pot, combine the eggplant, tomato, onion, garlic, tomato paste, sugar, olive oil, water, vinegar, salt, and pepper. Mix well.

2. Secure the lid on the pot. Close the pressure-release valve. Select MANUAL and set the pot at HIGH pressure for 2 minutes. At the end of the cooking time, allow the pot to sit undisturbed for 5 minutes, then quick-release any remaining pressure. Select CANCEL.

3. Select SAUTÉ/NORMAL. Cook, stirring frequently, until the caponata is thick and caramelized, 3 to 5 minutes. Stir in the capers and olives.

4. Transfer to a serving bowl or platter. Top with the parsley and toasted nuts, if using.

NOTE: All the vegetables will release enough water for your pot to come to pressure. Note that water content in vegetables can vary, so if you're nervous about this, use ¼ cup water during the pressure-cooking phrase, especially if you have an 8-quart Instant Pot.

Smoky Eggplant Dip

This dish is typically made by smoking and charring the eggplant on a stovetop. It makes an ungodly mess, to tell you the truth. It's a lot cleaner if you allow the eggplant to char a little as I've described below in order to make this restaurant favorite at home.

ACTIVE TIME	FUNCTION	RELEASE	TOTAL TIME
25 minutes	Sauté (Normal); Manual (High)	Quick	40 minutes

Egg-Free, Nut-Free, Dairy-Free, Vegan • 10 Ingredients or Less • SERVES 4

⅓ cup vegetable oil

1 medium eggplant, peeled, halved, and sliced crosswise

½ onion, diced

3 cloves garlic, minced

¼ teaspoon ground turmeric

⅛ teaspoon cayenne pepper

½ teaspoon kosher salt

⅓ cup diced tomato

½ cup water

¼ teaspoon liquid smoke

2 tablespoons chopped fresh cilantro, for garnish

Naan, for serving

1. Select SAUTÉ/NORMAL on the Instant Pot. When the pot is hot, add 3 tablespoons of the vegetable oil. Once the oil is hot, add as many eggplant slices as will fit in a single layer. (You won't be able to get all the slices in at once. Once the first round of slices shrinks, you can add more slices to the pot. Eggplant is porous and sucks up a lot of oil. Add the additional 2 tablespoons oil when needed.) Do not turn the eggplant until the first side is properly charred. Use a spatula or spoon and scrape up the char from the bottom of the pot as needed. It will take 10 to 15 minutes to get all the eggplant charred.

2. Once all of the eggplant is charred and softened, add the onion, garlic, turmeric, cayenne, and salt. Allow the spices to roast in the oil, gently stirring, for 30 seconds to 1 minute.

3. Add the tomato and stir, scraping up every last bit of the browned bits from the bottom of the pot. Add the water, and close the pot immediately before you lose any liquid through evaporation.

4. Secure the lid on the pot. Close the pressure-release valve. Select MANUAL and set the pot at HIGH pressure for 3 minutes. At the end of the cooking time, use a quick release to depressurize.

5. Stir in the liquid smoke. Allow the mixture to cool slightly so that it thickens up a bit before serving.

6. Transfer to a serving bowl, garnish with the cilantro, and serve with naan.

Eggplant Parmigiana Pasta

I posted this recipe in my Facebook group as a thank-you to the great folks in there, and the response was overwhelmingly positive. The really nice thing about it is that the eggplant takes on a variety of flavors and almost disappears in the dish, making it a great way to sneak some veggies into the picky eaters at your dinner table.

ACTIVE TIME	FUNCTION	RELEASE	TOTAL TIME
10 minutes	Manual (High)	Natural + Quick	37 minutes

Egg-Free, Nut-Free · SERVES 6 to 8

4 cups peeled, chopped eggplant

1 (14-ounce can) diced tomatoes

1½ cups water

1 cup diced onion

3 tablespoons unsalted butter or vegetable oil

3 cloves garlic, minced

1 tablespoon tomato paste

1 tablespoon dried Italian seasoning

1½ teaspoons kosher salt

1 teaspoon red pepper flakes

9 ounces penne pasta (2 cups)

½ cup bread crumbs

⅓ cup shredded Parmesan cheese

1½ cups (8-ounce tub) small mozzarella balls (bocconcini)

1. In the Instant Pot, combine the eggplant, tomatoes, water, onion, 2 tablespoons of the butter, garlic, tomato paste, Italian seasoning, salt, and red pepper flakes. Stir to combine.

2. Add the pasta, and stir. I know it doesn't loock like there will be enough water to cook the pasta. But #trustUrvashi, because the vegetables will release a lot of water. Secure the lid on the pot. Close the pressure-release valve. Select MANUAL and set the pot at HIGH pressure for 7 minutes. At the end of the cooking time, allow the pot to sit undisturbed for 10 minutes, then quick-release any remaining pressure.

3. Meanwhile, in a small skillet, melt the remaining 1 tablespoon butter over medium heat. Add the bread crumbs and mix well. Remove from the heat; allow to cool. Mix with the Parmesan cheese and set aside.

4. Preheat the broiler. Add the mozzarella balls to the pasta, and transfer the pasta to a casserole dish. Sprinkle with the bread crumb mixture and broil for 2 to 3 minutes. Serve.

Hot-and-Sour Soup

If you knew how much starch there was in prepared hot-and-sour soup, you might pause for a moment. I prefer to make my own at home. I find that tofu doesn't do very well under pressure, so I often add it at the end of the recipe, as I did here.

ACTIVE TIME	FUNCTION	RELEASE	TOTAL TIME
10 minutes	Manual (High); Sauté (Normal)	Natural + Quick	35 minutes

Nut-Free, Dairy-Free, Gluten-Free, Low-Carb • 10 Ingredients or Less • SERVES 4

5 cups mushroom broth or water

1 cup dried wood ear mushrooms, broken into very small pieces

1 (8-ounce) can sliced water chestnuts, undrained

1 (8-ounce) can sliced bamboo shoots, undrained

¼ cup gluten-free soy sauce

2 tablespoons Chinese black vinegar or white vinegar

2 tablespoons rice vinegar or white vinegar

2 teaspoons kosher salt

1 teaspoon black pepper

1 pound extra-firm tofu, cut into 1-inch cubes

4 large eggs, lightly beaten

½ cup chopped green onions

1. In the Instant Pot, combine the broth, mushrooms, water chestnuts, bamboo shoots, soy sauce, Chinese black vinegar, rice vinegar, salt, and pepper. Stir to combine.

2. Secure the lid on the pot. Close the pressure-release valve. Select MANUAL and set the pot at HIGH pressure for 5 minutes. At the end of the cooking time, allow the pot to sit undisturbed for 10 minutes, then quick-release any remaining pressure.

3. Select SAUTÉ/NORMAL.

4. Add the tofu. Slowly pour in the eggs. Mix three times around the pot with chopsticks. Cover the pot and let the eggs cook in the broth for 1 minute. Select CANCEL.

5. Ladle the soup into bowls, garnish with the green onions, and serve.

NOTE: Treat this recipe as a guideline and season to taste. Use vinegar for tang and black pepper for spice. Add one or both until the soup tastes right to you.

Mushroom Stroganoff

You won't miss the meat in this dish at all. I am not a fan of using meat substitutes, because I really feel like vegetables have so much lovely favor on their own. This stroganoff will show you how easy it is to modify traditional meat-based dishes into their vegetarian counterparts.

ACTIVE TIME	FUNCTION	RELEASE	TOTAL TIME
10 minutes	Manual (High)	Natural + Quick	30 minutes

Egg-Free, Nut-Free • 10 Ingredients or Less • SERVES 4

1 cup diced onion

3 cloves garlic, minced

1 (10-ounce) package frozen mixed mushrooms or 1½ cups sliced mixed fresh mushrooms

2 tablespoons butter or olive oil

1 tablespoon Dijon mustard

1 tablespoon soy sauce

1 teaspoon kosher salt

1 teaspoon black pepper

1¼ cups water

8 ounces fusilli or other pasta (about 2 cups)

½ cup sour cream

½ cup shredded Parmesan cheese

½ cup chopped fresh parsley

1. In the Instant Pot, combine the onion, garlic, mushrooms, butter, mustard, soy sauce, salt, pepper, water, and pasta. Stir well to combine.

2. Secure the lid on the pot. Close the pressure-release valve. Select MANUAL and set the pot at HIGH pressure for 5 minutes. At the end of the cooking time, allow the pot to sit undisturbed for 5 minutes, then quick-release any remaining pressure.

3. Open the lid, stir in the sour cream, Parmesan cheese, and parsley, and serve.

Mushroom-Mascarpone Pasta

My husband and I almost got into a fight when I made this. He was supposed to photograph it, and he looked at it and said, "You used a can of mushroom soup?" Does the man not know me? OF COURSE NOT! This is the dish that will convince you never need to use a can of mushroom soup again. Serve with a simple salad and some crusty bread on the side to sop up all the sauce.

ACTIVE TIME	FUNCTION	RELEASE	TOTAL TIME
15 minutes	Sauté (Normal); Manual (High)	Natural + Quick	35 minutes

Egg-Free, Nut-Free • 10 Ingredients or Less • SERVES 4

2 tablespoons butter

3 cloves garlic, minced

1 teaspoon dried thyme

½ teaspoon red pepper flakes

1 cup chopped onion

8 ounces cremini mushrooms, trimmed and sliced

1 teaspoon kosher salt

1 teaspoon black pepper

1¾ cups water

8 ounces fettuccine, broken in half

8 ounces mascarpone cheese

1 cup shredded Parmesan cheese

2 teaspoons fresh thyme leaves, for garnish (optional)

1. Select SAUTÉ/NORMAL on the Instant Pot. When the pot is hot, add the butter. Once the butter is melted, add the garlic, thyme, and red pepper flakes and cook for about 30 seconds.

2. Add the onion, mushrooms, salt, pepper, and water; stir to combine. Add the fettuccine, pushing it down into the liquid. Add the mascarpone on top of the pasta; do not stir.

3. Secure the lid on the pot. Close the pressure-release valve. Select MANUAL and set the pot at HIGH pressure for 5 minutes. At the end of the cooking time, allow the pot to sit undisturbed for 5 minutes, then quick-release any remaining pressure.

4. Open the lid and stir. Stir in the Parmesan cheese.

5. Divide the pasta among four dishes, garnish with the thyme, if desired, and serve.

Buttery Whipped Potatoes with Cabbage

Half gone. In ten minutes. Seriously. Half of it was gone in ten minutes and there were only three people in my house the day I tested it. I don't know why this super-simple combination of potatoes and cabbage is so comforting, creamy, and delicious—but it is. I urge you to make this dish immediately. You may like it better than your usual mashed potatoes.

ACTIVE TIME	FUNCTION	RELEASE	TOTAL TIME
15 minutes	Manual (High)	Natural + Quick	40 minutes

Egg-Free, Nut-Free, Gluten-Free • 10 Ingredients or Less • SERVES 10

4 cups peeled and cubed (2-inch) russet potatoes

2½ teaspoons kosher salt

1½ cups water

3 cups coarsely chopped cabbage

⅓ cup heavy cream

4 tablespoons (½ stick) unsalted butter, plus additional melted butter for serving

½ teaspoon black pepper

¼ teaspoon ground nutmeg

1 cup chopped green onions

1. In the Instant Pot, combine the potatoes, 1 teaspoon of the salt, and the water.

2. Place the cabbage in a 6×3-inch round baking pan. Place a trivet on top of the potatoes. Place the pan on the trivet.

3. Secure the lid on the pot. Close the pressure-release valve. Select MANUAL and set the pot at HIGH pressure for 5 minutes. At the end of the cooking time, allow the pot to sit undisturbed for 10 minutes, then quick-release any remaining pressure. Remove the pan with the cabbage and set aside. Drain the potatoes.

4. In a stand mixer fitted with the paddle attachment, combine the potatoes, cream, butter, the remaining 1½ teaspoons salt, pepper, and nutmeg. Whip until creamy. (You can also use a hand mixer and whip the potatoes in the pot.)

5. Stir in the cooked cabbage and the green onions.

6. To serve, make a well in the center of each serving and fill with melted butter.

LENTILS, BEANS & LEGUMES

HOW TO COOK BEANS IN THE INSTANT POT

Before we start to talk about how to cook these, there are a few terms we should get straight.

Beans, lentils, legumes, pulses, dal . . . what do all these terms mean?

Legumes refer to plants whose fruit is enclosed in a pod. There are more than 13,000 varieties and these include fresh soybeans, fresh beans, peanuts, etc.

Pulses are the dried seeds of legumes. So, all pulses are legumes, but not all legumes are pulses. Examples include chickpeas, dried soybeans, mung beans, and kidney beans.

"Dal" is a term that is used to describe beans and lentils, and often split lentils or split beans.

One Bean, Four Lives

Most beans can be used in one of four ways: whole, split with skin, split without skin, and ground. As a cook, knowing which form you're using is important because it affects cooking times.

As a rule of thumb for pressure cookers, whole beans take 30 minutes, split beans (such as split peas, red lentils, etc.) take between 3 and 10 minutes, and ground beans, such as chickpea flour, are used in batters.

What this means is that you can choose to substitute whole beans for other whole beans in these recipes, if you are looking to experiment. Substituting pinto beans for kidney beans will work without any changes to cooking times. But if you substitute red kidney beans (30 minutes) for red lentils (3 minutes), your results will be terrible.

What Are Heirloom Beans and Do I Need Them?

"Heirloom" basically means that those beans are genetically different in that they haven't been crossbred with any other varietal or species of beans. Do you need them? I find them to be slightly fuller flavored, but the best part is that they're often variegated, speckled, and just pretty-looking. But they all cook up the same. The variety is intriguing and fun, but no, you

▸ French Lentils

▸ Cannellini

▴ Black-Eyed Peas

▸ 15-Bean Mix

◂ Pinto Beans

▴ Adzuki Beans

▴ Brown lentils

◂ Navy Beans

▾ Mung Beans

▴ Lima Beans

▴ Chickpeas

don't have to use heirloom beans to find nutritious, good-for-you sources of protein and fiber.

Do I Have to Soak Beans for Pressure Cooking?

This is a question with no clear answer. Some people do, and others don't. I do a hybrid method, and I will explain why. Note that you never need to soak beans such as red or yellow lentils and split peas.

All the recipes in this book were tested with beans soaked in very hot water for one hour. This is why I do this. If I write a recipe for kidney beans to cook for thirty minutes, and you use beans that are very, very old, it will take longer than thirty minutes. Then you will think I gave you a bad recipe, and worse, dinner will be late.

I don't know about you, but most days I can barely remember how old *I* am, let alone how old the beans in my pantry are. I also don't know whether they arrived in my pantry as old beans or young beans.

I find it best to soak whole beans. In your cooking you can prepare beans in one of five ways. I have listed them in order of prettiest resultant beans and most even cooking to—well, they're cooked but they're not pretty. Note also that longer soak times lead to a better breakdown of the indigestible sugars in the bean, so it's easier on your stomach as well.

Various Ways to Soak Beans for the Instant Pot

1. **Overnight:** Soak 1 cup beans in 3 to 4 cups water overnight. Drain the beans and use as directed. If you are soaking for longer than 8 hours, place the beans in the refrigerator, otherwise you'll be dealing with semifermented beans.

2. **Overnight-freezer method:** This isn't really a different method but rather a clever hack my husband, Roger, suggested that worked really well. When you're soaking overnight as listed above, soak twice as many beans as the recipe calls for. In the morning, put half the soaked beans into a zip-top bag and place the bag in the freezer. I found that with this method, I didn't even have to defrost the beans, I just threw the frozen beans in the Instant Pot and cooked the recipes as written. I love this sort of #ruthlessefficiency, don't you?

3. **Hot water method:** Soak 1 cup beans in 3 to 4 cups very hot water (preferably boiling water) for an hour. The beans will have plumped and absorbed almost all the water in this time. Drain the beans and use as directed. This is what I did for all the bean recipes in this book. The beans cook consistently with very little breaking. This is my preferred last-minute method.

4. **Pressure-cooker soaking:** Place 1 cup beans and 3 to 4 cups water in the Instant Pot. Close the lid. Set the pot to MANUAL on HIGH for 0 minutes (yes, 0 minutes, that's a thing). Allow the pot to rest undisturbed for 15 minutes to release pressure naturally, then quick-release any remaining pressure. Drain the beans and use as directed. This method is very like the hot water method—you're just using the pressure cooker to heat the water for you. Note that beans are more likely to burst open with this method of soaking, so you could be trading beauty for convenience here.

5. **Don't soak:** That's right, be a maverick! In this case, I suggest you add 5 to 10 minutes to the cooking time under pressure. You may need to add a little more water as well. Note that this may adversely affect the other ingredients in the recipe. It is also more likely to cause gastric distress for some people, and your beans will be more likely to split and not be pretty. I suggest you do this only after you're really comfortable working with different types of beans. For what it's worth, I never cook them this way. But your mileage may vary, and this may well be your favorite method.

Should I Salt the Beans While Soaking?

Salting the beans, especially if you plan to use the pressure cooker soaking method, helps keep the beans from splitting. I do not salt my beans when soaking because I try to eat less salt as a rule, and when I'm cooking a dish, it's hard for me to estimate how much salt to add if I'm using beans soaked in salted water. You can choose to add salt to the soaking water if you wish. I know many of you will have heard that salting beans before cooking makes them tougher, but most people now agree that is not the case. And salting them before cooking allows the salt to penetrate the beans, making them more flavorful. Throughout the book, I have listed that first dash of salt as optional, since some of you may need to watch your sodium intake carefully. But if that's not a pressing concern, I suggest you add that salt.

Keep in mind that all these recipes ask you to add salt for cooking anyway, which I think lends a lovely flavor to the beans.

How Long Do I Cook Beans in the Instant Pot?

There are many charts available on how long to cook various beans, but here are the rules of thumb I start with:

- Smaller lentils or split legumes such as split green peas, black lentils, brown lentils, etc., are in the 2 to 5 minutes camp. Split garbanzos (chickpeas or chana dal) should be cooked up to 10 minutes if you want them to disintegrate into the dish.
- Smaller beans such as black-eyed peas, navy beans, and whole green mung beans should be cooked for 10 minutes under pressure.
- Large whole beans such as black beans, kidney beans, pinto beans, etc., should be cooked for 30 to 40 minutes. If you want tender but whole beans, 30 minutes will work. For beans that need to cook down into the soup, you may want to do 40 or even 50 minutes.

What this means is that you can mix and match beans, at least with respect to cooking times.

- Any split dal recipe will work with another
- Any small bean recipe will work with another
- Any large whole bean recipe will work with another

So, feel free to experiment on a day when you're not rushing around trying to get dinner on the table quickly. It's always easy to recook undercooked beans, so start on the lower end of the scale and add time as needed.

Beans in Pounds, Cups, and Cans

Usually a 1-pound bag of beans contains 2½ to 3 cups dried beans. This will, of course, depend on how big or small the beans are, but that's a good rule of thumb to start with.

- A 15-ounce can is equivalent to about 1½ cups cooked beans, or about ¾ cup dried beans.
- Beans will double or triple in volume when cooked, so 1 cup dried beans will yield almost 3 cups cooked beans. Smaller beans like black-eyed peas tend to double, but larger beans like chickpeas tend to triple, so 1 cup dried beans will yield about 2 cups cooked black-eyed peas but closer to 3 cups cooked chickpeas.
- Because beans will double or triple in volume once cooked, be careful not to overfill your Instant Pot.

Spicy Coconut-Chickpea Curry

I love coconut anything. This chickpea curry is both sweet and spicy at the same time. It tastes great fresh but is also fantastic as leftovers. You could make a pot of brown rice on top of the curry, ending up with rice and chickpeas ready at the same time.

ACTIVE TIME	FUNCTION	RELEASE	TOTAL TIME
20 minutes	Sauté (Normal); Manual (High)	Natural	1 hour 10 minutes

Egg-Free, Nut-Free, Dairy-Free, Gluten-Free, Vegan • 10 Ingredients or Less • SERVES 6

For the Coconut Paste

1 cup chopped fresh cilantro

½ cup unsweetened shredded coconut

8 cloves garlic, minced

1 (2-inch) piece fresh ginger, sliced

1 serrano pepper, stemmed

½ cup water

For the Curry

2 tablespoons olive oil

1 tomato, diced

1½ teaspoons kosher salt

1 teaspoon ground turmeric

½ to 1 teaspoon cayenne pepper

1 cup dried chickpeas, soaked and drained (see page 108)

1½ cups water

Cooked rice or naan, for serving

1. **For the coconut paste:** In a blender, combine the cilantro, coconut, garlic, ginger, serrano, and water. Blend until you have a rough, gritty mixture, about 30 seconds.

2. **For the curry:** Select SAUTÉ/NORMAL on the Instant Pot. When the pot is hot, add the olive oil. Once the oil is hot, add the coconut mixture and cook 2 minutes, stirring constantly, until lightly toasted.

3. Add the tomato, salt, turmeric, and cayenne. Cook, stirring frequently, until the tomatoes have softened, about 2 minutes. Add the chickpeas and water. Select CANCEL.

4. Secure the lid on the pot. Close the pressure-release valve. Select MANUAL and set the pot at HIGH pressure for 30 minutes (for chickpeas with a little bite) or 40 minutes (for super-soft chickpeas).

5. At the end of the cooking time, use a natural release to depressurize.

6. Serve with rice or naan.

Chickpeas in Spicy Tomato Sauce with Brown Rice

This is Indian chana masala and rice in one go. How is that not just #ruthlessefficiency at its best? You must use brown rice for this dish, since white rice would cook too quickly and dry out in the time it would take for the chickpeas to finish cooking. You can serve this dish with rice, naan, or even buttered rolls—my favorite accompaniment to these chickpeas.

ACTIVE TIME	FUNCTION	RELEASE	TOTAL TIME
15 minutes	Manual (High)	Natural + Quick	1 hour 5 minutes

Egg-Free, Nut-Free, Dairy-Free, Gluten-Free, Vegan · SERVES 6

For the Rice

1 cup brown rice, rinsed and drained

1 tablespoon vegetable oil or Ghee (page 240)

1 teaspoon kosher salt

1 cup water

For the Chickpeas

1 cup coarsely chopped onion

1 cup coarsely chopped tomato

8 cloves garlic, peeled

1 tablespoon minced fresh ginger

1 small jalapeño pepper, minced

2 teaspoons garam masala

2 teaspoons prepared chana masala spice blend

2 teaspoons kosher salt

1 teaspoon ground turmeric

½ to 1 teaspoon cayenne pepper

1. For the rice: In a 6×3-inch round baking pan, combine the rice, oil, salt, and water. Stir well to combine; set aside. (You do not need to cover.)

2. For the chickpeas: In a food processor, combine the onion, tomato, garlic, and ginger. Process until finely chopped.

3. In the Instant Pot, combine the onion mixture, jalapeño, garam masala, chana masala spice blend, salt, turmeric, cayenne, chickpeas, and water. Stir to combine. Place a tall trivet in the pot over the chickpeas. Place the pot with the rice on the trivet.

4. Secure the lid on the pot. Close the pressure-release valve. Select MANUAL and set the pot at HIGH pressure for 30 minutes. At the end of the cooking time, allow the pot to sit undisturbed for 10 minutes, then quick-release any remaining pressure.

1 cup dried chickpeas, soaked and drained (see page 108)

1½ cups water

1 tablespoon tamarind extract

¼ cup chopped fresh cilantro (optional)

5. Carefully remove the rice. Use the back of a spoon to mash half the chickpeas until thickened. Stir in the tamarind extract.

6. Serve the chickpeas with the rice. Garnish with cilantro, if using.

Chickpeas in Spicy Tomato Sauce with Brown Rice (page 114)

Spiced Red Lentils

One day I will figure out how to make authentic-tasting Ethiopian injera bread in a few hours rather than a week. But until then, I keep making many Ethiopian dishes to go with this much-awaited injera. This simple dish can be eaten with any bread of your choice or with plain steamed rice.

ACTIVE TIME	FUNCTION	RELEASE	TOTAL TIME
10 minutes	Manual (High)	Natural + Quick	40 minutes

Egg-Free, Nut-Free, Dairy-Free, Gluten-Free, Vegan • 10 Ingredients or Less • **SERVES 4**

1 cup dried red lentils, rinsed and drained

½ cup chopped onion

1 tablespoon minced fresh ginger

3 cloves garlic, minced

1 teaspoon kosher salt

1 teaspoon ground turmeric

1 teaspoon paprika

2 tablespoons Niter Kibbeh (page 241), Ghee (page 240), or vegetable oil, plus additional for finishing (optional)

1. In a 6×3-inch round baking pan, combine the lentils, onion, ginger, garlic, salt, turmeric, paprika, and niter kibbeh.

2. Pour 1½ cups water into the Instant Pot. Place a trivet in the pot. Place the pan on the trivet.

3. Secure the lid on the pot. Close the pressure-release valve. Select MANUAL and set the pot at HIGH pressure for 10 minutes. At the end of the cooking time, allow the pot to sit undisturbed for 10 minutes, then quick-release any remaining pressure.

4. Stir in additional niter kibbeh, if desired, and serve.

Tangy Mung Bean Stew

Tangy, spicy, hearty mung bean stew is a great accompaniment to the Cumin-Cardamom Rice with Peas and Carrots (page 171). It works well as leftovers and also freezes very well.

ACTIVE TIME	FUNCTION	RELEASE	TOTAL TIME
15 minutes	Manual (High)	Natural + Quick	45 minutes

Egg-Free, Nut-Free, Dairy-Free, Gluten-Free, Vegan · SERVES 6

1 cup whole green mung beans

1 cup diced onion

1 cup diced carrots

3 cloves garlic, minced

1 tablespoon minced fresh ginger

1 tablespoon tamarind paste

1 serrano pepper, minced

1 teaspoon ground turmeric

1 teaspoon ground cumin

1 teaspoon ground coriander

1 teaspoon kosher salt

½ teaspoon ground cinnamon

4 cups water

For Tempering

3 tablespoons Ghee (page 240) or vegetable oil

1 tablespoon cumin seeds

6 cloves garlic, thinly sliced

Naan or cooked rice, for serving

1. In the Instant Pot, combine the mung beans, onion, carrots, garlic, ginger, tamarind paste, serrano, turmeric, cumin, coriander, salt, cinnamon, and water.

2. Secure the lid on the pot. Close the pressure-release valve. Select MANUAL and set the pot at HIGH pressure for 10 minutes. At the end of the cooking time, allow the pot to sit undisturbed for 10 minutes, then quick-release any remaining pressure.

3. Open the lid and use the back of a spoon to mash some of the beans to thicken the stew.

4. **For tempering:** In a small pan or a tadka ladle, heat the ghee. When the ghee is melted, add the cumin seeds and allow them to sizzle for about 30 seconds. Add the garlic and let it sizzle, but be careful not to burn it. Pour the mixture into the stew and mix well.

5. Serve with naan or rice.

Texas Caviar

Not a fish egg in sight in this dish. I'm not sure why it's called caviar, but it is a staple at picnics in Texas. I love the fresh burst of flavors from the vegetables. I prefer to serve this at room temperature so that you can taste all the different flavors in this dish.

ACTIVE TIME	FUNCTION	RELEASE	TOTAL TIME
20 minutes	Manual (High)	Natural + Quick	50 minutes plus 1 hour standing time

Egg-Free, Nut-Free, Dairy-Free, Gluten-Free, Vegan • 10 Ingredients or Less • SERVES 6

¼ cup olive oil

3 tablespoons apple cider vinegar, plus more to taste

2 tablespoons fresh lemon juice, plus more to taste

2 teaspoons kosher salt

1 teaspoon ground cumin

½ teaspoon ancho chile powder

1 cup dried black-eyed peas

2 cups water

2 cups fresh or frozen corn kernels

1 cup diced red onion

2 cups halved cherry tomatoes

½ cup chopped fresh cilantro

1 to 2 tablespoons minced jalapeño pepper

1. In a small bowl, whisk together the olive oil, vinegar, lemon juice, salt, cumin, and chile powder. Set aside.

2. In the Instant Pot, combine the black-eyed peas and water.

3. Secure the lid on the pot. Close the pressure-release valve. Select MANUAL and set the pot at HIGH pressure for 10 minutes. At the end of the cooking time, allow the pot to sit undisturbed for 10 minutes, then quick-release any remaining pressure.

4. Open the lid and stir in the corn. Close the lid and allow the corn to cook in the residual heat, about 5 minutes; drain.

5. Once the mixture has cooled, add the onion, tomatoes, cilantro, and jalapeño. Pour in the dressing and mix well. Add additional lemon juice and vinegar to taste.

6. Allow the salad to stand for 1 hour or so before serving at room temperature.

Chipotle Chili with Zucchini, Corn, and Fire-Roasted Tomatoes (page 124)

Chipotle Chili with Zucchini, Corn, and Fire-Roasted Tomatoes

Vegetarian chili recipes are a dime a dozen, I know, but I use the same base recipe for my cook-off-winning keto chili in this bean chili. Starting with your own spices makes a world of difference. You can use black beans, large white beans, red kidney beans, or any combination you prefer for this recipe.

ACTIVE TIME	FUNCTION	RELEASE	TOTAL TIME
10 minutes	Manual (High)	Natural + Quick	1 hour 15 minutes

Egg-Free, Nut-Free, Dairy-Free, Gluten-Free, Vegan · SERVES 6

1 cup chopped onion

1 cup canned fire-roasted tomatoes

2 cloves garlic, minced

3 corn tortillas, torn into large pieces

1 tablespoon chopped canned chipotle chile in adobo sauce

1 tablespoon Mexican red chili powder

2 teaspoons ground cumin

2 teaspoons kosher salt

1 teaspoon dried oregano

1 cup water

½ cup dried pinto beans, soaked and drained (see page 108)

2 cups frozen corn kernels, thawed

2 cups chopped zucchini

OPTIONAL TOPPINGS: Sour cream, pickled jalapeños, chopped fresh cilantro, shredded sharp cheddar cheese, chopped red onion

1. In a blender, combine the onion, tomatoes, garlic, tortillas, chipotle chile, chili powder, cumin, salt, and oregano. Blend until smooth.

2. Transfer the sauce to the Instant Pot. Pour the water into the blender jar and slosh it around to get the last of the sauce; add to the pot. Stir in the pinto beans.

3. Secure the lid on the pot. Close the pressure-release valve. Select MANUAL and set the pot at HIGH pressure for 35 minutes. At the end of the cooking time, allow the pot to sit undisturbed for 10 minutes, then quick-release any remaining pressure.

4. Open the lid and stir in the corn and zucchini. Close the lid and allow the corn and zucchini to cook in the residual heat for about 10 minutes.

5. Serve with optional toppings, if desired.

Pinto Pozole Stew

I call for canned hominy here because dried hominy isn't that easy to come by for many people. I love that it still maintains a chewy texture at the end of cooking. If you want a softer texture for the beans and hominy, cook for an additional ten minutes. You can use an immersion blender at the end to break up some of the beans and hominy to slightly thicken the stew.

ACTIVE TIME	FUNCTION	RELEASE	TOTAL TIME
10 minutes	Manual (High)	Natural + Quick	1 hour

Egg-Free, Nut-Free, Dairy-Free, Gluten-Free, Vegan • 10 Ingredients or Less • SERVES 4

1 (25-ounce) can Mexican-style hominy, drained

1 cup dried pinto beans, soaked and drained (see page 108)

1 onion, chopped

3 cloves garlic, minced

2 canned chipotle chiles in adobo sauce, chopped, plus 1½ teaspoons sauce from the can

2 teaspoons ground cumin

2 teaspoons ancho chile powder

1½ teaspoons kosher salt

1 teaspoon dried oregano

2 cups water

Juice of 1 lemon

¼ cup chopped fresh cilantro

OPTIONAL TOPPINGS: Sour cream, shredded cabbage, chopped onion, sliced radishes, avocado slices, corn chips

1. In the Instant Pot, combine the hominy, pinto beans, onion, garlic, chipotle chiles and adobo sauce, cumin, chile powder, salt, oregano, and water.

2. Secure the lid on the pot. Close the pressure-release valve. Select MANUAL and set the pot at HIGH pressure for 30 minutes. At the end of the cooking time, allow the pot to sit undisturbed for 10 minutes, then quick-release any remaining pressure.

3. Stir in the lemon juice and cilantro.

4. Serve with optional toppings, if desired.

Pinto Pozole Stew (page 125)

Chili-Spiced Pinto Beans in Red Sauce

I don't know what to call these because they don't taste like the traditional beans in most Mexican restaurants—can I just say, I think they taste BETTER? But they are most definitely Mexican-inspired beans, so here you have pinto beans in a red sauce. Serve with Mexican Red Rice (page 168) for a complete protein.

ACTIVE TIME	FUNCTION	RELEASE	TOTAL TIME
10 minutes	Manual (High)	Natural + Quick	1 hour

Egg-Free, Nut-Free, Dairy-Free, Gluten-Free, Vegan • 10 Ingredients or Less • SERVES 4

1 (14.5-ounce) can diced tomatoes

1 cup dried pinto beans, soaked and drained (see page 108)

1 small onion, chopped

3 cloves garlic, minced

2 tablespoons vegetable oil

2 tablespoons tomato paste

1 tablespoon Mexican red chili powder

2 teaspoons ground cumin

1½ teaspoons kosher salt

1½ cups water

¼ cup chopped pickled jalapeños

½ cup chopped fresh cilantro

Queso fresco, for serving (optional)

1. In the Instant Pot, combine the tomatoes, pinto beans, onion, garlic, oil, tomato paste, chili powder, cumin, salt, and water.

2. Secure the lid on the pot. Close the pressure-release valve. Select MANUAL and set the pot at HIGH pressure for 30 minutes. At the end of the cooking time, allow the pot to sit undisturbed for 10 minutes, then quick-release any remaining pressure.

3. Stir in the jalapeños and cilantro. Top servings with queso fresco, if desired.

Peanut-Sauced Veggies and Black-Eyed Peas

Peanut butter with black-eyed peas? What madness is this? Well, everyone who has made this will tell you—it's a delicious, hearty, inexpensive madness that you should indulge in often.

ACTIVE TIME	FUNCTION	RELEASE	TOTAL TIME
10 minutes	Manual (High)	Natural + Quick	45 minutes

Egg-Free, Dairy-Free, Gluten-Free, Vegan • 10 Ingredients or Less • SERVES 6

1 cup chopped onion

1 cup canned diced tomatoes

1 cup dried black-eyed peas, soaked and drained

1 (12-ounce) package frozen chopped spinach

1 large sweet potato, diced (about 1½ cups)

1 teaspoon kosher salt

1 teaspoon black pepper

2½ cups water

¼ cup peanut butter

1. In the Instant Pot, combine the onion, tomatoes, black-eyed peas, spinach, sweet potato, salt, pepper, and water.

2. Add the peanut butter to the top of the mixture; do not stir in. (Be sure that everything, including the peanut butter, is submerged under the liquid. This is to prevent the peanut butter from sticking to the pot and burning.)

3. Secure the lid on the pot. Close the pressure-release valve. Select MANUAL and set the pot at HIGH pressure for 15 minutes. At the end of the cooking time, allow the pot to sit undisturbed for 10 minutes, then quick-release any remaining pressure.

4. Stir to combine, and serve.

Collard Greens and Red Bean Stew

This hearty dish is inspired by a Georgian dish called *lobio* that's flavored with blue fenugreek leaves—which are impossible to come by in my little suburban town. I decided to try this with frozen collard greens instead to add a touch of bitterness. This makes a humble-looking dish that will surprise you with a slight hint of sweet among the savory.

ACTIVE TIME	FUNCTION	RELEASE	TOTAL TIME
5 minutes	Manual (High)	Natural + Quick	1 hour 10 minutes

Egg-Free, Nut-Free, Dairy-Free, Gluten-Free, Vegan • 10 Ingredients or Less • SERVES 4

1 cup dried red beans, soaked and drained (see page 108)

1 cup frozen chopped collard greens

1 cup chopped onion

3 cloves garlic, minced

3 bay leaves

¼ cup chopped fresh cilantro

2 tablespoons balsamic vinegar

1 teaspoon ground cumin

1 teaspoon kosher salt

1 teaspoon black pepper

1¾ cups water

1. In the Instant Pot, combine the red beans, collard greens, onion, garlic, bay leaves, cilantro, vinegar, cumin, salt, pepper, and water.

2. Secure the lid on the pot. Close the pressure-release valve. Select MANUAL and set the pot at HIGH pressure for 40 minutes. At the end of the cooking time, allow the pot to sit undisturbed for 15 minutes, then quick-release any remaining pressure.

3. Open the lid, remove the bay leaves, and use the back of a spoon to mash some of the beans to thicken the stew.

4. Serve with buttered rolls or bread.

Black Bean Soup

Here is a simple black bean soup that you can serve with Mexican Red Rice (page 168) for a complete meal. Feel free to swap out any other whole beans for the black beans in this recipe.

ACTIVE TIME	FUNCTION	RELEASE	TOTAL TIME
10 minutes	Manual (High)	Natural + Quick	1 hour 10 minutes

Egg-Free, Nut-Free, Dairy-Free, Gluten-Free, Vegan • SERVES 4

1 cup dried black beans, soaked and drained (see page 108)

1 onion, diced

1 stemmed, seeded, and roughly chopped red, yellow, or orange bell pepper

1 jalapeño pepper, minced

4 cloves garlic, minced

½ bunch cilantro, chopped

2 teaspoons kosher salt

2 teaspoons dried oregano

1 teaspoon dried thyme

2 teaspoons ground cumin

2 bay leaves

2 cups water

½ cup chopped green onions, for garnish

1. In the Instant Pot, combine the black beans, onion, bell pepper, jalapeño, garlic, cilantro, salt, oregano, thyme, cumin, bay leaves, and water.

2. Secure the lid on the pot. Close the pressure-release valve. Select MANUAL and set the pot at HIGH pressure for 30 minutes. At the end of the cooking time, allow the pot to sit undisturbed for 15 minutes, then quick-release any remaining pressure.

3. Remove the bay leaves. Using an immersion blender, purée some of the soup to thicken it while leaving most of the beans whole for texture.

4. Ladle the soup into bowls, garnish with the green onions, and serve.

**Mixed-Bean
Burrito Bowls**

(page 134)

Mixed-Bean Burrito Bowls

These remind me of the burrito bowls at Chipotle, except without the meat. I love the efficiency of being able to make rice, beans, and vegetables all in one go. This will freeze and reheat very well, so make lots and enjoy.

ACTIVE TIME	FUNCTION	RELEASE	TOTAL TIME
20 minutes	Manual (High)	Natural + Quick	1 hour 10 minutes

Egg-Free, Nut-Free, Gluten-Free • SERVES 6

1 (14-ounce) can fire-roasted tomatoes

1 cup chopped onion

½ green bell pepper, stemmed, seeded, and roughly chopped

½ jalapeño pepper, sliced

4 cloves garlic, chopped

1 or 2 canned chipotle chiles in adobo sauce

2 teaspoons kosher salt

1 teaspoon ground cumin

1 teaspoon Mexican red chili powder

½ cup dried red beans, soaked and drained (see page 108)

½ cup dried cannellini beans, soaked and drained (see page 108)

½ cup brown rice, rinsed and drained

½ cup water

2 cups frozen or fresh corn kernels

1 (8-ounce) container crumbled feta cheese

½ cup chopped fresh cilantro

1. In a blender, combine the tomatoes, onion, bell pepper, jalapeño, garlic, chipotle chiles, salt, cumin, and chili powder. Blend until smooth.

2. In the Instant Pot, combine the tomato mixture, red beans, cannellini beans, rice, and water.

3. Secure the lid on the pot. Close the pressure-release valve. Select MANUAL and set the pot at HIGH pressure for 30 minutes. At the end of the cooking time, allow the pot to sit undisturbed for 10 minutes, then quick-release any remaining pressure.

4. Open the lid and stir in the corn. Close the lid and allow the corn to cook in the residual heat for 2 to 3 minutes.

5. Stir in the feta cheese and cilantro. Serve with optional toppings, if desired.

NOTE: You can use 1 cup of either red beans or cannellini beans instead of ½ cup of each, if you prefer.

OPTIONAL TOPPINGS: Shredded lettuce or cabbage, chopped red onion, avocado slices, pico de gallo, sour cream, shredded cheese

Smoky Red Bean–Vegetable Stew

This soup looks simple, but the smoked paprika adds such a lovely depth to this dish. I like to cook it for forty minutes to get a thick, chunky stew. Add a salad and a few pieces of toasted, buttered bread or a bowl of rice, and you're good to go.

ACTIVE TIME	FUNCTION	RELEASE	TOTAL TIME
15 minutes	Sauté (Normal); Manual (High)	Natural + Quick	1 hour 15 minutes

Egg-Free, Nut-Free, Dairy-Free, Gluten-Free, Vegan • 10 Ingredients or Less • SERVES 6

2 tablespoons vegetable oil

2 cups chopped carrots

2 cups stemmed, seeded, and roughly chopped green bell peppers

1 cup chopped tomato

1 cup chopped onion

¾ cup chopped fresh cilantro or parsley

¼ cup chopped fresh mint

3 cloves garlic, minced

1 cup dried red beans, soaked and drained (see page 108)

2 tablespoons smoked paprika

1 to 1½ teaspoons kosher salt

1 teaspoon black pepper

1½ cups water

1. Select SAUTÉ/NORMAL on the Instant Pot. When the pot is hot, add the oil. Once the oil is hot, add the carrots, bell peppers, tomato, onion, ½ cup of the cilantro, mint, and garlic. Cook, stirring frequently, until the vegetables soften, about 2 minutes. Select CANCEL.

2. Add the red beans, paprika, salt, pepper, and water. Stir well to combine.

3. Secure the lid on the pot. Close the pressure-release valve. Select MANUAL and set the pot at HIGH pressure for 40 minutes. At the end of the cooking time, allow the pot to sit undisturbed for 10 minutes, then quick-release any remaining pressure.

4. Open the lid and use the back of a spoon to mash some of the beans to thicken the stew.

5. Ladle the stew into bowls, garnish with the remaining ¼ cup cilantro, and serve.

Smoky Red Bean-Vegetable Stew (page 135)

Cumin-Scented Black Beans and Rice

This recipe is inspired by Cuban black beans and rice (*moros y cristianos*, literally "Moors and Christians") but is much simpler because the beans and rice are cooked at the same time. It took a little trial and error for me to make them simultaneously. I'll be honest—it doesn't look the same as the traditional dish because the rice and the beans both tend to darken rather than having pure white rice and black beans—but it tastes the same.

ACTIVE TIME	FUNCTION	RELEASE	TOTAL TIME
15 minutes	Sauté (Normal); Manual (High)	Natural	1 hour 10 minutes

Egg-Free, Nut-Free, Dairy-Free, Gluten-Free, Vegan • 10 Ingredients or Less • **SERVES 6**

2 tablespoons vegetable oil

1 cup chopped onion

1 cup stemmed, seeded, and roughly chopped green bell pepper

1 small jalapeño pepper, minced

3 cloves garlic, minced

2 tablespoons ground cumin

1 tablespoon plus 1½ teaspoons tomato paste

1 tablespoon dried oregano

2 bay leaves

2 teaspoons kosher salt

1 cup brown rice, rinsed and drained

1 cup dried black beans, soaked and drained (see page 108)

1¾ cups water

¼ cup chopped fresh cilantro, for garnish (optional)

1. Select SAUTÉ/NORMAL on the Instant Pot. When the pot is hot, add the oil. Once the oil is hot, add the onion, bell pepper, jalapeño, and garlic. Cook until the vegetables just soften, 1 minute.

2. Add the cumin, tomato paste, oregano, bay leaves, and salt. Add the rice, black beans, and water. Stir well to combine. Select CANCEL.

3. Secure the lid on the pot. Close the pressure-release valve. Select MANUAL and set the pot at HIGH pressure for 35 minutes. At the end of the cooking time, use a natural release to depressurize.

4. Remove the bay leaves. Serve the beans and rice garnished with the cilantro, if desired.

Black Bean Tortilla Soup

Don't forgo the few minutes spent caramelizing the chipotle chile–tomato mix in this recipe—it makes a world of difference in the final taste of this soup. I usually set out a variety of toppings, allowing guests to customize their soup.

ACTIVE TIME	FUNCTION	RELEASE	TOTAL TIME
20 minutes	Sauté (Normal); Manual (High)	Natural	1 hour 5 minutes

Egg-Free, Nut-Free, Dairy-Free, Gluten-Free, Vegan • 10 Ingredients or Less • SERVES 4

1 cup chopped tomato

½ cup roughly chopped onion

2 cloves garlic, minced

1 canned chipotle chile in adobo sauce, plus 1 teaspoon sauce from the can

½ jalapeño pepper

¼ cup fresh cilantro leaves

1 teaspoon kosher salt

1 tablespoon vegetable oil

2 corn tortillas, torn into small pieces (optional)

1 cup dried black beans, soaked and drained (see page 108)

4 cups water

1 cup frozen corn kernels

OPTIONAL TOPPINGS: **Toasted tortilla strips, grated cheese, avocado slices, sour cream**

1. In a blender, combine the tomato, onion, garlic, chipotle chile and adobo sauce, jalapeño, cilantro, and salt. Blend until smooth.

2. Select SAUTÉ/NORMAL on the Instant Pot. When the pot is hot, add the oil. Once the oil is hot and shimmering, pour in the tomato mixture and cook, stirring frequently, until the sauce is thickened, 10 minutes.

3. Add the tortillas, if desired (to thicken the soup), black beans, and water.

4. Secure the lid on the pot. Close the pressure-release valve. Select MANUAL and set the pot at HIGH pressure for 25 minutes. At the end of the cooking time, use a natural release to depressurize.

5. Open the lid and stir in the corn. Allow the corn to cook in the residual heat, about 5 minutes.

6. Serve with optional toppings, if desired.

Harissa Bean Stew

The homemade harissa paste in this dish takes less than five minutes to make, will last for months, and is an excellent addition to soups. It's all spice with no tomatoes, so do not substitute commercial harissa for this, as it will taste quite different. In place of the fresh onion, carrot, and celery, you can use a 14-ounce package of frozen mirepoix for faster prep.

ACTIVE TIME	FUNCTION	RELEASE	TOTAL TIME
15 minutes	Manual (High)	Natural + Quick	1 hour 5 minutes

Egg-Free, Nut-Free, Dairy-Free, Gluten-Free, Vegan • 10 Ingredients or Less • SERVES 6

1½ cups dried 15-bean mix, soaked and drained (see page 108)

1 cup canned diced tomatoes

1 cup chopped carrots

1 cup chopped onion

1 cup chopped celery

1 to 2 tablespoons Harissa (see page 242)

1 teaspoon ground turmeric

1 teaspoon kosher salt

½ teaspoon black pepper

2½ cups water

2 tablespoons apple cider vinegar

½ cup chopped fresh parsley

1. In the Instant Pot, combine the bean mix, tomatoes, carrots, onion, celery, harissa, turmeric, salt, pepper, and water.

2. Secure the lid on the pot. Close the pressure-release valve. Select MANUAL and set the pot at HIGH pressure for 30 minutes. At the end of the cooking time, allow the pot to sit undisturbed for 10 minutes, then quick-release any remaining pressure.

3. To thicken the soup, puree it with an immersion blender or mash some of the beans with the back of a spoon.

4. Stir in the vinegar and parsley and serve.

Creamy Greek Gigantes Beans

It took me longer to find these beans than it took me to make the dish. You can get them online or in some health food stores. Look for large dried lima beans if you can't find gigantes beans. Creamy and delicious, they really benefit from a last-minute drizzle of olive oil.

ACTIVE TIME	FUNCTION	RELEASE	TOTAL TIME
15 minutes	Sauté (Normal); Manual (High)	Quick	1 hour 5 minutes

Egg-Free, Nut-Free, Dairy-Free, Vegan • 10 Ingredients or Less • SERVES 4

2 tablespoons extra-virgin olive oil, plus additional for drizzling

1 cup chopped onion

3 cloves garlic, minced

1 cup dried gigantes beans or large lima beans, soaked and drained (see page 108)

1 (14.5-ounce) can diced tomatoes

1½ teaspoons kosher salt

1 teaspoon dried oregano

½ teaspoon ground thyme

½ teaspoon red pepper flakes

2 bay leaves

1½ cups water

½ cup chopped fresh parsley, for garnish

Crusty bread, for serving

1. Select SAUTÉ/NORMAL on the Instant Pot. When the pot is hot, add the olive oil. Once the oil is hot, add the onion and garlic and cook, stirring frequently, 1 to 2 minutes.

2. Add the gigantes beans, tomatoes, salt, oregano, thyme, red pepper flakes, bay leaves, and water. Stir well to combine. Select CANCEL.

3. Secure the lid on the pot. Close the pressure-release valve. Select MANUAL and set the pot at HIGH pressure for 45 minutes. At the end of the cooking time, use a quick release to depressurize.

4. Open the lid, remove the bay leaves, and use the back of a spoon to mash some of the beans to thicken the mixture.

5. Ladle the beans into bowls, drizzle with olive oil, and sprinkle with the parsley. Serve with bread.

Lemony Lima–Navy Bean Soup

Until I first had this dish, I didn't see what the fuss was about. The list of ingredients looks so simple. Somehow, they all work well together and you end up with a comforting, filling soup.

ACTIVE TIME	FUNCTION	RELEASE	TOTAL TIME
15 minutes	Manual (High)	Natural + Quick	1 hour 5 minutes

Egg-Free, Nut-Free, Dairy-Free, Gluten-Free, Vegan • 10 Ingredients or Less • SERVES 6

1 (12-ounce) package frozen lima beans

1 cup dried navy beans, soaked and drained (see page 108)

1 cup chopped onion

3 large carrots, peeled and cut into 2-inch pieces

1 cup chopped celery

3 cloves garlic, minced

1½ teaspoons dried rosemary

1 teaspoon kosher salt

3 cups water

2 tablespoons fresh lemon juice

2 tablespoons extra-virgin olive oil

¼ cup chopped fresh parsley, for garnish (optional)

1. In the Instant Pot, combine the lima beans, navy beans, onion, carrots, celery, garlic, rosemary, salt, and water.

2. Secure the lid on the pot. Close the pressure-release valve. Select MANUAL and set the pot at HIGH pressure for 30 minutes. At the end of the cooking time, allow the pot to sit undisturbed for 10 minutes, then quick-release any remaining pressure.

3. Stir in the lemon juice and olive oil. Ladle the soup into bowls, garnish with the parsley, if desired, and serve.

Boston Baked Beans

These beans are so delicious! No one will know you didn't spend all day simmering them in an oven. The best part? You can make these and the Boston Brown Bread (page 225) at the same time. Just put the ingredients for the beans in the pot. Place a tall trivet in the pot, place the covered pan with the bread batter on it, and cook them both for 40 minutes instead of 30, and you'll have a two-for-one dish.

ACTIVE TIME	FUNCTION	RELEASE	TOTAL TIME
5 minutes	Manual (High)	Natural + Quick	55 minutes

Egg-Free, Nut-Free, Dairy-Free • 10 Ingredients or Less • SERVES 4

1 cup dried navy beans, soaked and drained (see page 108)

1 cup diced onion

½ cup ketchup

3 tablespoons molasses

1 tablespoon yellow mustard

1 tablespoon Worcestershire sauce

2 bay leaves

1½ teaspoons kosher salt

1 teaspoon black pepper

1 cup water

1. In the Instant Pot, combine the navy beans, onion, ketchup, molasses, mustard, Worcestershire sauce, bay leaves, salt, pepper, and water. Stir well to combine.

2. Secure the lid on the pot. Close the pressure-release valve. Select MANUAL and set the pot at HIGH pressure for 30 minutes. At the end of the cooking time, allow the pot to sit undisturbed for 10 minutes, then quick-release any remaining pressure.

3. Remove the bay leaves, use the back of a spoon to mash some of the beans to thicken the dish, and serve.

Simple Adzuki Beans and Sticky Rice

Combining red beans and rice and cooking them at the same time took a little experimenting. My first few attempts either had too much or too little water. This version works well, and in one fell swoop, you've got a wonderful rice-and-bean dish that's also quite pretty. I like to start with a little miso soup, and then serve this along with Crispy Sesame-Ginger Broccoli from my *Air Fryer Revolution* cookbook.

ACTIVE TIME	FUNCTION	RELEASE	TOTAL TIME
10 minutes	Manual (High)	Quick	55 minutes

Egg-Free, Nut-Free, Dairy-Free, Gluten-Free, Vegan • 10 Ingredients or Less • SERVES 4

For the First Cooking Cycle

½ cup dried adzuki beans, soaked and drained (see page 108)

1 teaspoon kosher salt

2 cups water

For the Second Cooking Cycle

1 cup glutinous rice, rinsed and drained

2 tablespoons black sesame seeds, for garnish

1. **For the first cooking cycle:** In the Instant Pot, combine the adzuki beans, salt, and water.

2. Secure the lid on the pot. Close the pressure-release valve. Select MANUAL and set the pot at HIGH pressure for 20 minutes. At the end of the cooking time, use a quick release to depressurize. Drain the beans, reserving the water. Measure out 1 cup of the reserved water; discard the rest.

3. **For the second cooking cycle:** Return the bean mixture to the pot. Add the rice and the 1 cup reserved bean-cooking water.

4. Secure the lid on the pot. Close the pressure-release valve. Select MANUAL and set the pot at HIGH pressure for 4 minutes. At the end of the cooking time, use a quick release to depressurize.

5. Spoon the beans and rice into bowls, sprinkle with the sesame seeds, and serve.

White Bean–Potato Soup with Sauerkraut

I keep a small jar of sauerkraut in the fridge just to make this soup. It's so fast and easy, and the tang of the sauerkraut along with the creaminess of the beans and potatoes makes it a fast, comforting dish. Serve this with bread and butter for a simple meal.

ACTIVE TIME	FUNCTION	RELEASE	TOTAL TIME
10 minutes	Manual (High)	Natural + Quick	1 hour

Egg-Free, Nut-Free, Dairy-Free, Gluten-Free, Vegan • 10 Ingredients or Less • SERVES 6

2 cups whole baby red potatoes

1 cup dried cannellini beans, soaked and drained (see page 108)

3 large carrots, peeled and cut into 2-inch pieces

1 cup sauerkraut, with brine

3 bay leaves

1 cup chopped onion

3 cloves garlic, minced

1 teaspoon kosher salt

1 teaspoon black pepper

3½ cups water, plus more, if needed

1. In the Instant Pot, combine the potatoes, cannellini beans, carrots, sauerkraut, bay leaves, onion, garlic, salt, pepper, and water.

2. Secure the lid on the pot. Close the pressure-release valve. Select MANUAL and set the pot at HIGH pressure for 30 minutes. At the end of the cooking time, allow the pot to sit undisturbed for 10 minutes, then quick-release any remaining pressure.

3. Open the lid, remove the bay leaves, and use the back of a spoon to mash some of the beans to thicken the soup. Add water, if needed, to thin the texture. Serve.

Cajun Red Beans

I have added a can of beans to this recipe so that you can get some thickness from them as they cook down—since this is how these beans are typically made at home. You can, of course, choose to omit them. If you would rather use only dried beans, increase the quantity of dried beans to 1½ cups and purée all but 1 cup of the cooked beans. Alternatively, purée a can of kidney beans and add at the end.

ACTIVE TIME	FUNCTION	RELEASE	TOTAL TIME
10 minutes	Manual (High); Sauté (Normal)	Natural + Quick	1 hour 10 minutes

Egg-Free, Nut-Free, Dairy-Free, Gluten-Free, Vegan • SERVES 6

1 cup dried kidney beans, soaked and drained (see page 108)

1 cup diced tomatoes, fresh or canned

½ cup diced onion

½ cup diced celery

½ cup stemmed, seeded, and roughly chopped green bell pepper

3 cloves garlic, minced

2 teaspoons Cajun seasoning

½ teaspoon dried thyme

½ teaspoon dried sage

1 teaspoon kosher salt

2 teaspoons Louisiana hot sauce

2 cups water

1 (16-ounce) can Creole cream-style red beans

2 teaspoons liquid smoke

Cooked rice, for serving

1. In the Instant Pot, combine the kidney beans, tomatoes, onion, celery, bell pepper, garlic, Cajun seasoning, thyme, sage, salt, hot sauce, and water.

2. Secure the lid on the pot. Close the pressure-release valve. Select MANUAL and set the pot at HIGH pressure for 35 minutes. At the end of the cooking time, allow the pot to sit undisturbed for 15 minutes, then quick-release any remaining pressure.

3. Select SAUTÉ/NORMAL on the pot. Add the red beans, if using, and stir in the liquid smoke. Cook, stirring frequently, until thick and bubbling, about 10 minutes.

4. Serve over rice.

RICE & GRAINS

PERFECT PRESSURE-COOKER RICE

Rice is probably the most commonly cooked food all over the world, and yet many of us still struggle to cook the perfect pot of it. I will share what I have learned through research and lots of trial and error to help you cook the perfect rice in the Instant Pot.

To do that, it is important to first understand the different types of rice, their distinguishing characteristics, and the best uses for each type.

How to Think About Rice

Rice has two types of starches.

- There's **amylopectin,** which makes rice sticky. Glutinous rice and Arborio rice are high in amylopectin, as are sushi rice and sweet rice.
- **Amylose** is a longer type of starch that doesn't bind or stick together.

It is the balance of these two elements that defines whether the rice grains stick together or each grain cooks up separately.

The following factors also affect cooking times and the nature of the finished product.

- **Grain length/starch quantity:** Rice is distinguished by the length of the grain and the dominant type of starch in it. Some rice, like basmati, is long and skinny and contains amylose. Other rice, like sushi, jasmine, or some brown rice, is short and fat and contains amylopectin.
- **Color:** You'll find rice in many colors—black, brown, white, and red—and different colors carry very different textures and flavors.
- **Aroma:** Basmati rice has kind of a popcorn aroma, jasmine has a floral aroma, and brown rice has a great nutty scent.

So the different types of rice aren't always interchangeable and can't be swapped out for one another.

▾ Brown Rice

▴ Black Rice

▾ Quinoa

▾ Wild Rice Blend

► Sweet Rice

▴ Buckwheat

► Millet

◄ Farro

◄ Barley

► Basmati Rice

Different Types of Rice

Here are a few guidelines to help you pick the correct type of rice for your dish. These are just guidelines, not rules, so at the end of the day, use whatever you like and enjoy it!

- **Basmati rice** doesn't get fatter as it cooks, it gets thinner and longer. I wish I were like this after a few cupcakes too many.
- **Jasmine rice** is a sticky rice, which means cooked grains will stick together, making it great to eat with chopsticks.
- **Brown rice** is believed to be healthier than white rice, but it's really not that much better for you. Brown rice is all-purpose rice and usually tastes nuttier and is chewier than white rice.
- **Black rice** has a coating that contains the same chemical as the skin of an eggplant. This chemical is how both black rice and eggplant gain their color.
- **Sushi rice** is very sticky, which is why it's great for sushi rolls.
- **Glutinous rice** is not high in gluten as the name might suggest. It's just really sticky (and yummy).

Choosing the Right Type of Rice

As you can see from the list above, you should choose the type of rice depending on the dish you're making.

When you're making an Indian or Middle Eastern dish like biryani or pilau, you'll want a basmati or long grain to ensure that the grains will separate and not clump together.

On the other hand, if you're making Asian dishes that you would use chopsticks for and need the rice to be a little sticky, you would choose jasmine. I also love jasmine rice with Thai curries cooked with coconut milk, as the jasmine rice and coconut flavors pair so well together.

Brown rice is nutty and chewy and a good all-purpose rice. As noted, it's traditionally been considered healthier than white rice, but that's debatable since it has only a little more fiber and can carry more contaminants if it's not organic. But it cooks really well in a pressure cooker, so it's fine to substitute for white rice if you prefer the taste or texture.

Black rice, once known as "forbidden rice" because it was so extravagant only royalty ate it, has a bran hull that gives it its dark purple color. This rice is used for puddings and is quite sticky once the hull is broken. Stickier kinds of rice have the ability to raise your blood sugar more than a longer-grain, less-sticky rice like basmati would.

Sushi rice is very sticky and starchy due to its high level of amylopectin. If you're watching your blood sugar, please note that the starchier the rice, the more it will raise it—so this one might be one to avoid.

Ironically, glutinous rice such as Arborio has no gluten in it. This rice is the most sticky and is used for dishes such as puddings or risotto.

All of these rices have a different type and level of starch, which is the most important aspect to note.

Long-, Medium-, and Short-Grain Rice

Long-grain rice grows to about four times its length when cooked. Medium-grain rice grows about two times its size, and short-grain rice stays short but plumps up when cooking.

Why Pressure-Cook Rice?

Now that we've discussed how to pick the best rice for your dish, let's discuss why you should cook it in a pressure cooker.

Rice tastes so much different and better when cooked in the pressure cooker than in stovetop methods, but you don't want to just take your stovetop method and put it into a pressure cooker. The pressure cooker changes the chemistry of food and how the food reacts.

The pressure cooker prepares rice in a much different way than stovetop cooking.

1. **Creamier mouthfeel:** The heat and moisture in a pressure cooker gelatinizes the starch in rice for a much creamier mouthfeel. For basmati, which shouldn't get creamy, it cooks the rice the whole way through for nicely separated grains of rice.

2. **Better aroma:** Cooking rice in a pressure cooker requires less water because there is no evaporation as in the stovetop method. One of the key benefits of cooking in a pressure cooker is that none of the aroma of the rice is lost, and it turns out so much more flavorful.

3. **Hands-free:** You don't have to babysit rice in the pressure cooker, nor do you have to presoak the rice, resulting in less time and effort for you.

How Much Water to Use When Making Rice

It may surprise you to know that for all rice other than black and Arborio, the ratio of water to rice is 1:1. For Arborio and black rice, the ratio will be 1 cup rice to 1½ cups water.

With brown, red, and mixed rice, the water and rice ratios remain the same, but the natural pressure-release time needs to be 22 minutes,

Cooking Times for Rice

	BASMATI, JASMINE, GLUTINOUS	ARBORIO	BROWN, RED, MIXED	BLACK
INGREDIENTS	1 CUP RICE: 1 CUP WATER	1 CUP RICE: 1½ CUPS WATER, PLUS MORE LIQUID AFTER COOKING	1 CUP RICE: 1 CUP WATER	1 CUP RICE: 1½ CUPS WATER, PLUS MORE LIQUID AFTER COOKING
TIME	4 TO 5 MINUTES, 10 NATURAL PRESSURE RELEASE	5 MINUTES, 10 NATURAL PRESSURE RELEASE	22 MINUTES, 10 NATURAL PRESSURE RELEASE	22 MINUTES, 10 NATURAL PRESSURE RELEASE

not just 10. I know that we were all taught differently, but remember that pressure cooking is very different from stovetop cooking.

Why is it so different and why is it so much quicker? Because you don't lose water to evaporation in pressure cooking, you don't need more water for more fibrous rice like brown rice. However, brown, black, and red rice do require longer cooking times because the water needs more time to penetrate the outer husk. Be sure to be patient and let the pressure release naturally when your rice is done, because that's actually time that the rice is cooking. If you quick-release the cooker, the rice won't be cooked all the way through.

It's important to note that for all rice, I recommend rinsing it and draining off all the water prior to putting it in the pressure cooker.

Troubleshooting Rice in a Pressure Cooker

Of course, not everyone likes their rice exactly the same way, and mistakes can always occur in cooking, so below is a list of how to troubleshoot common rice issues.

- If the rice is too mushy, reduce the water; then, if need be, reduce the time.
- If it's too chewy, try increasing the cooking time first. If that doesn't work, try increasing the liquid.
- If the center of the rice is hard but the outer portion isn't, try increasing the water by a tad and, if need be, increase the cooking time.
- Always ensure you're doing a ten-minute NPR (natural pressure release).
- If the rice is sticking to the bottom, try adding ghee or butter first, then reduce the cooking and NPR time, or try using a ceramic liner.

Lebanese Lentils and Rice

Call it *kushari*, *mujadara*, *khichidi*, or lentils and rice—many cultures have some version of this dish. I love the Lebanese/Greek version, but when I've tried it in the past, the lentils and rice cook at different speeds, so you end up having to cook them separately or suffer undercooked lentils or overcooked rice. I was determined to cook this as a one-pot, one-step dish and use the Instant Pot to do it so I didn't have to stand and stir while it cooked. This recipe succeeds in doing just that.

ACTIVE TIME	FUNCTION	RELEASE	TOTAL TIME
15 minutes	Sauté (Normal); Manual (High)	Natural + Quick	45 minutes

Egg-Free, Nut-Free, Dairy-Free, Gluten-Free, Vegan • 10 Ingredients or Less • SERVES 6

⅓ cup dried brown lentils

2 tablespoons Ghee (page 240) or vegetable oil

1 large yellow onion, sliced

1 teaspoon kosher salt, plus more to taste

1 cup basmati rice, rinsed and drained

½ teaspoon ground cumin

½ teaspoon ground coriander

2 cups water

1. Place the lentils in a small bowl. Cover with hot water and soak for 15 to 20 minutes; drain.

2. Select SAUTÉ/NORMAL on the Instant Pot. When the pot is hot, add the ghee. Once the ghee is melted, add the onion. Season with a little salt and cook, stirring, until the onions begin to crisp around the edges but are not burned, 5 to 10 minutes. (If you have the time, you can keep cooking them until they are well browned.) Remove half the onions from the pot and reserve as a garnish. Select CANCEL.

3. Add the lentils, rice, cumin, coriander, salt, and water. Stir well to combine.

4. Secure the lid on the pot. Close the pressure-release valve. Select MANUAL and set the pot at HIGH pressure for 6 minutes. At the end of the cooking time, allow the pot to sit undisturbed for 10 minutes, then quick-release any remaining pressure.

5. Transfer to a serving dish. Sprinkle with the reserved cooked onions and serve.

Greek Spinach and Rice

This sounds very simple, and it is indeed simple to make, but it does pack a lot of nutrition and taste into a side dish. You may want to stir in some halved cherry tomatoes for a pop of color and taste at the end, but it's also great just by itself. Sometimes I mix a cup of cooked chickpeas into the rice and eat that for a light meal.

ACTIVE TIME	FUNCTION	RELEASE	TOTAL TIME
15 minutes	Sauté (Normal); Manual (High)	Natural + Quick	40 minutes

Egg-Free, Nut-Free, Dairy-Free, Gluten-Free, Vegan • 10 Ingredients or Less • **SERVES 4**

2 tablespoons olive oil

2 cups chopped spring onions or green onions

3 cloves garlic, minced

1½ cups packed chopped fresh spinach

1 cup basmati rice, rinsed and drained

¼ cup chopped fresh dill

1 tablespoon tomato paste

1 teaspoon kosher salt

1 cup water

1 tablespoon red wine vinegar

1. Select SAUTÉ/NORMAL on the Instant Pot. When the pot is hot, add the olive oil. Once the oil is hot, add the onions and garlic and cook for about 30 seconds.

2. Stir in the spinach, rice, dill, tomato paste, salt, and water. Select CANCEL.

3. Secure the lid on the pot. Close the pressure-release valve. Select MANUAL and set the pot at HIGH pressure for 4 minutes. At the end of the cooking time, allow the pot to sit undisturbed for 10 minutes, then quick-release any remaining pressure.

4. Stir in the vinegar and serve.

Jeweled Coconut Rice

This makes a very pretty dish. It can be served as a sweet rice side dish or as a dessert-like snack. Do not add the sugar before the rice is cooked. I've tried that, and not only is it likely to burn, it also doesn't allow the rice to cook properly. Stir the sugar into the finished rice to make an easy glaze that just melts into the rice.

ACTIVE TIME	FUNCTION	RELEASE	TOTAL TIME
10 minutes	Manual (High)	Natural + Quick	35 minutes

Egg-Free, Nut-Free, Dairy-Free, Gluten-Free, Vegan • 10 Ingredients or Less • SERVES 4

1 cup basmati rice, rinsed and drained

½ cup mixed dried fruit

½ cup unsweetened shredded coconut

½ cup shredded carrot

1 cup water

2 tablespoons granulated sugar

½ cup toasted cashews and walnuts, for garnish (optional)

1. In the Instant Pot, combine the rice, dried fruit, coconut, carrot, and water. Stir well.

2. Secure the lid on the pot. Close the pressure-release valve. Select MANUAL and set the pot at HIGH pressure for 4 minutes. At the end of the cooking time, allow the pot to sit undisturbed for 10 minutes, then quick-release any remaining pressure.

3. Stir in the sugar. Divide among individual plates, garnish with the toasted cashews and walnuts, if desired, and serve.

Mexican Red Rice

I made this dish a few times before I got it just right with respect to both ease and taste. After much experimenting, I found this worked better with tomato paste than with fresh tomatoes. I'm sure you've read about how tomato paste burns in the Instant Pot, but that's only true if you don't have enough water. This rice is flavorful and easy.

ACTIVE TIME	FUNCTION	RELEASE	TOTAL TIME
10 minutes	Manual (High)	Natural + Quick	35 minutes

Egg-Free, Nut-Free, Dairy-Free, Gluten-Free, Vegan • 10 Ingredients or Less • SERVES 6

1 cup basmati rice, rinsed and drained

1 cup diced onion

½ to 1 jalapeño pepper, minced

3 cloves garlic, minced

1 tablespoon tomato paste

1 tablespoon vegetable oil

2 teaspoons ground cumin

1 teaspoon Goya Sazón with cilantro and achiote (optional)

1 cup water

¼ cup chopped fresh cilantro, for garnish

1. In the Instant Pot, combine the rice, onion, jalapeño, garlic, tomato paste, oil, cumin, Sazón (if using), and water.

2. Secure the lid on the pot. Close the pressure-release valve. Select MANUAL and set the pot at HIGH pressure for 4 minutes. At the end of the cooking time, allow the pot to sit undisturbed for 10 minutes, then quick-release any remaining pressure.

3. Transfer to a serving dish, garnish with the cilantro, and serve.

Cumin-Cardamom Rice with Peas and Carrots

So simple. So pretty. And such a perfect accompaniment for every Indian curry you make. I like being able to use frozen veggies for dishes, since not only are they nutritious and easy with no prep but they also make last-minute meals a lot easier to put together.

ACTIVE TIME	FUNCTION	RELEASE	TOTAL TIME
10 minutes	Sauté (Normal); Manual (High)	Natural + Quick	35 minutes

Egg-Free, Nut-Free, Dairy-Free, Gluten-Free, Vegan • 10 Ingredients or Less • SERVES 8

For the Whole Garam Masala

2 tablespoons Ghee (page 240) or vegetable oil

4 green cardamom pods

4 whole cloves

8 black peppercorns

1 (2- to 3-inch) piece Indian cinnamon stick (cassia bark)

1 or 2 black cardamom pods (optional)

For the Rice

1 teaspoon cumin seeds

1 cup chopped green onions

2 cups basmati rice, rinsed and drained

1 teaspoon kosher salt

2 cups water

1 (10-ounce) package frozen peas and carrots

1. **For the whole garam masala:** Select SAUTÉ/NORMAL on the Instant Pot. When the pot is hot, add the ghee. Once the ghee is melted, add the green cardamom pods, cloves, peppercorns, cassia bark, and black cardamom pods, if using. Stir well. Allow the spices to sizzle for about 30 seconds.

2. **For the rice:** Stir in the cumin seeds, green onions, rice, salt, and water. Gently add the peas and carrots on top of the rice. Do not stir.

3. Secure the lid on the pot. Close the pressure-release valve. Select MANUAL and set the pot at HIGH pressure for 4 minutes. At the end of the cooking time, allow the pot to sit undisturbed for 10 minutes, then quick-release any remaining pressure.

4. Using a very light hand, mix the peas and carrots and rice. Transfer to a large serving dish or platter.

NOTE: If desired, you can use 1 teaspoon ground garam masala in place of the whole garam masala ingredients. If using ground garam masala, omit the green cardamom pods, cloves, peppercorns, cassia bark, and black cardamom pods. Heat the ghee in the Instant Pot. Once the ghee is melted, add the ground garam masala with the cumin seeds, green onions, and remaining rice ingredients.

Curried Vegetable Rice

Here's an easy vegetables-and-rice dish, and you can always add cooked chickpeas or cooked black-eyed peas at the end. I like it as a change of pace from a typical rice with veggies recipe.

ACTIVE TIME	FUNCTION	RELEASE	TOTAL TIME
10 minutes	Manual (High)	Natural + Quick	35 minutes

Egg-Free, Nut-Free, Dairy-Free, Gluten-Free, Vegan • 10 Ingredients or Less • SERVES 4

2 cups shredded green cabbage

1 (10-ounce) package frozen peas and carrots

1 cup basmati rice, rinsed and drained

1 cup stemmed, seeded, and roughly chopped red bell pepper

2 tablespoons vegetable oil

2 vegetable bouillon cubes, crushed

1 teaspoon curry powder

1 teaspoon kosher salt

½ teaspoon dried thyme

1 cup water

1. In the Instant Pot, combine the cabbage, peas and carrots, rice, bell pepper, oil, bouillon cubes, curry powder, salt, thyme, and water. Stir well.

2. Secure the lid on the pot. Close the pressure-release valve. Select MANUAL and set the pot at HIGH pressure for 4 minutes. At the end of the cooking time, allow the pot to sit undisturbed for 10 minutes, then quick-release any remaining pressure.

3. Gently stir before serving.

Sesame-Ginger Rice Porridge

This is my take on the classic and very comforting Chinese porridge called congee. I know you're going to think—just looking at the recipe—that it calls for too much ginger. I had several people test it, and they all agreed—it is just the right amount. This is one of those universal comfort-food tastes, no matter where you grew up. Perfect for cold days, or days you don't feel very well.

ACTIVE TIME	FUNCTION	RELEASE	TOTAL TIME
10 minutes	Manual (High)	Natural + Quick	50 minutes

Egg-Free, Nut-Free, Dairy-Free, Gluten-Free, Vegan • 10 Ingredients or Less • SERVES 4

1 cup glutinous rice or Arborio rice, rinsed and drained

2 cups chopped button or cremini mushrooms

¼ cup sliced fresh ginger

3 tablespoons toasted sesame oil

2 teaspoons kosher salt

6 cups water

½ cup chopped green onions

OPTIONAL TOPPINGS: Chopped roasted peanuts, tofu, corn, chili crisp, toasted sesame seeds, cooked and shelled edamame

1. In the Instant Pot, combine the rice, mushrooms, ginger, 1 tablespoon of the sesame oil, salt, and water.

2. Secure the lid on the pot. Close the pressure-release valve. Select MANUAL and set the pot at HIGH pressure for 20 minutes. At the end of the cooking time, allow the pot to sit undisturbed for 10 minutes, then quick-release any remaining pressure.

3. Stir vigorously to mash up some of the rice. (The congee thickens as it cools. You may need to add more water if you prefer a soupier congee.)

4. Stir in the green onions and the remaining 2 tablespoons sesame oil.

5. Serve with optional toppings, if desired.

Coconut Red Beans and Rice

I love the slight hint of coconut in this dish combined with the little bit of heat from the chile. If you like your food spicier, cut a slit into the pepper or chop it into four pieces before throwing it into the pot. Combine this with the Jamaican Mixed Vegetable Curry (page 57) and enjoy a simple, tasty meal.

ACTIVE TIME	FUNCTION	RELEASE	TOTAL TIME
5 minutes	Manual (High)	Natural + Quick	40 minutes

Egg-Free, Nut-Free, Dairy-Free, Gluten-Free, Vegan • 10 Ingredients or Less • SERVES 6

1 cup jasmine rice, rinsed and drained

1 Scotch bonnet or habanero chile pepper

3 sprigs fresh thyme or ½ teaspoon dried thyme

1 teaspoon kosher salt

½ teaspoon ground allspice

1 cup water

1 tablespoon Ghee (page 240), vegetable oil, or coconut oil

1 cup canned kidney beans, drained and rinsed

½ cup full-fat coconut milk

1. In the Instant Pot, combine the rice, chile pepper, thyme, salt, allspice, and water. Stir to combine. Add the ghee and stir to combine. Gently add the kidney beans on top of the rice; do not stir.

2. Secure the lid on the pot. Close the pressure-release valve. Select MANUAL and set the pot at HIGH pressure for 4 minutes. At the end of the cooking time, allow the pot to sit undisturbed for 10 minutes, then quick-release any remaining pressure.

3. Stir in the coconut milk. Place the lid back on the pot and allow to stand for 10 minutes.

4. Remove the thyme sprigs and the chile pepper and serve.

Rice and Lentil Porridge

Opinions are divided in my family about this—I think it's the epitome of comfort food. My husband likes it, but doesn't understand my "unreasonable passion" for it, as he puts it. I had this on our TwoSleevers South India culinary tour and thought it was the perfect thing, especially when topped with lots of ghee. You will have to make it and let me know if you're on Team Urvashi or Team Roger for this one.

ACTIVE TIME	FUNCTION	RELEASE	TOTAL TIME
10 minutes	Manual (High)	Natural + Quick	45 minutes

Egg-Free, Nut-Free, Dairy-Free, Gluten-Free • 10 Ingredients or Less • SERVES 4

½ cup short-grain rice, rinsed and drained

½ cup split moong dal, rinsed and drained

1 teaspoon kosher salt

3 cups water

2 tablespoons Ghee (page 240)

1 teaspoon black peppercorns

½ teaspoon mustard seeds

4 to 6 fresh curry leaves

1. In the Instant Pot, combine the rice, moong dal, salt, and water. Stir well.

2. Secure the lid on the pot. Close the pressure-release valve. Select MANUAL and set the pot at HIGH pressure for 15 minutes. At the end of the cooking time, allow the pot to sit undisturbed for 10 minutes, then quick-release any remaining pressure.

3. Open the lid and stir well. Use the back of a spoon to mash the rice and dal together. Add ½ cup more water, if desired, to get a very thick gruel-like consistency.

4. In a small pan or tadka ladle, heat the ghee over medium-high heat. Once the ghee is melted, add the peppercorns, mustard seeds, and curry leaves. Let them sputter and sizzle for 30 seconds.

5. Pour the spice mixture over the rice and dal and mix well. Serve hot.

Farro Risotto with Butternut Squash and Green Onions

I try to eat low-carb for the most part. I also give away a lot of the food that I test for recipes since I do a lot of cooking. Yeah, I didn't give this one away. I ate and ate and ate this—until it was all gone and I had a bit of a tummy ache! It is so good and just perfect for fall. It would make a great addition to your holiday table as well.

ACTIVE TIME	FUNCTION	RELEASE	TOTAL TIME
20 minutes	Sauté (Normal); Manual (High)	Natural + Quick	50 minutes

Egg-Free, Nut-Free • 10 Ingredients or Less • SERVES 4

1 cup pearled farro

3 tablespoons butter

3 cloves garlic, minced

1¼ cups chopped green onions

2 cups diced (½-inch) peeled butternut squash

1 teaspoon kosher salt

1 teaspoon black pepper

½ teaspoon dried thyme

1½ cups water

½ to ¾ cup shredded Parmesan cheese

1. Place the farro in a medium bowl. Cover with hot water and soak for 15 to 20 minutes; drain.

2. Select SAUTÉ/NORMAL on the Instant Pot. When the pot is hot, add 1 tablespoon of the butter. Once the butter is melted, add the garlic and allow it to sizzle for 5 to 10 seconds. Stir in 1 cup of the green onions. Select CANCEL.

3. Add the squash, farro, salt, pepper, thyme, and water.

4. Secure the lid on the pot. Close the pressure-release valve. Select MANUAL and set the pot at HIGH pressure for 10 minutes. At the end of the cooking time, allow the pot to sit undisturbed for 10 minutes, then quick-release any remaining pressure.

5. Add the Parmesan cheese and remaining 2 tablespoons butter. Lightly mash some of the farro and squash.

6. Serve garnished with the remaining ¼ cup green onions.

Farro-Bean Salad

The salad is delicious and fresh-tasting, but I don't mind admitting the beans and farro almost didn't make it as far as the salad bowl. I was quite surprised at how good just the salted farro and beans tasted by themselves! You could also make this with small navy beans, but do not substitute larger beans like kidney or pinto beans, as they won't cook in the same amount of time as the farro.

ACTIVE TIME	FUNCTION	RELEASE	TOTAL TIME
20 minutes	Manual (High)	Natural + Quick	50 minutes

Egg-Free, Nut-Free, Dairy-Free, Vegan • 10 Ingredients or Less • SERVES 4

½ cup pearled farro

½ cup dried black-eyed peas, soaked and drained

1 teaspoon kosher salt

1½ cups water

1 cup chopped fresh parsley

½ cup chopped green onions

½ cup cherry tomatoes, quartered

½ cup peeled diced cucumber

¼ cup olive oil

¼ cup chopped fresh mint

3 tablespoons fresh lemon juice

1. In the Instant Pot, combine the farro, black-eyed peas, salt, and water.

2. Secure the lid on the pot. Close the pressure-release valve. Select MANUAL and set the pot at HIGH pressure for 10 minutes. At the end of the cooking time, allow the pot to sit undisturbed for 10 minutes, then quick-release any remaining pressure. Drain off any excess water. Allow the farro-pea mixture to cool slightly.

3. Meanwhile, in a large bowl, mix together the parsley, green onions, tomatoes, cucumber, olive oil, mint, and lemon juice.

4. Add the farro and black-eyed peas, toss, and serve.

Kasha Pilaf with Cranberries, Kale, and Toasted Walnuts

I love the combination of textures and tastes in this pilaf—or is it a salad? The pleasantly chewy kasha, the soft, tart cranberries, the toasted, nutty walnuts, and the slightly bitter kale all combine to make a colorful and tasty dish. Add a fried egg on the side for each person, and dinner is served in a jiffy. Use the leftovers as a cold salad the next day with just a dash of vinegar and oil as an easy dressing.

ACTIVE TIME	FUNCTION	RELEASE	TOTAL TIME
15 minutes	Manual (High)	Natural + Quick	50 minutes

**Egg-Free, Dairy-Free, Gluten-Free, Vegan · 10 Ingredients or Less ·
SERVES 6 as a side dish; 4 as a main dish**

1 cup toasted buckwheat groats (kasha)

1 cup dried cranberries

2 teaspoons kosher salt

1 cup water

4 cups chopped kale

2 tablespoons olive oil

2 tablespoons orange zest

1 cup chopped walnuts, toasted

1. In the Instant Pot, combine the groats, cranberries, 1 teaspoon of the salt, and water.

2. Secure the lid on the pot. Close the pressure-release valve. Select MANUAL and set the pot at HIGH pressure for 15 minutes. At the end of the cooking time, allow the pot to sit undisturbed for 10 minutes, then quick-release any remaining pressure.

3. Meanwhile, in a large mixing bowl, combine the kale, olive oil, orange zest, and the remaining 1 teaspoon salt; mix with your hands, mashing and macerating the kale. (This will help soften the kale, reduce some of the bitterness, and allow the seasonings to penetrate.)

4. When the groats are cooked, fluff up the grains with a fork.

5. Divide the kale among plates; top with kasha and walnuts. (Or mix everything in one big bowl and serve.)

Cranberry-Millet Porridge (page 184)

Cranberry-Millet Porridge

Yet another use for the millet you will be using for the Cilantro-Lime Millet Pilaf (page 188). This dish is a great, creamy porridge, and the cranberries add a lovely sweetness. You will want to serve this hot, adding more milk or dairy-free alternatives as desired.

ACTIVE TIME	FUNCTION	RELEASE	TOTAL TIME
10 minutes	Manual (High)	Natural + Quick	45 minutes

Egg-Free, Nut-Free, Gluten-Free, Dairy-Free, Vegan • 10 Ingredients or Less • SERVES 4

½ cup millet

½ cup dried cranberries or raisins

1½ tablespoons granulated sugar

½ teaspoon ground cinnamon

1 cup water

1 cup heavy whipping cream, evaporated milk, or milk substitute, plus more for serving

1. In a 6×3-inch round baking pan, mix together the millet, cranberries, sugar, cinnamon, and water.

2. Pour the 1½ cups water into the Instant Pot. Place a trivet in the pot. Place the pan on the trivet.

3. Secure the lid on the pot. Close the pressure-release valve. Select MANUAL and set the pot at HIGH pressure for 15 minutes. At the end of the cooking time, allow the pot to sit undisturbed for 10 minutes, then quick-release any remaining pressure.

4. Carefully remove the millet porridge. Add the cream and stir hard to mix everything; slightly mash up the cranberries and millet as you stir.

5. Serve with additional cream.

Simple Wild Rice Pilaf

For this recipe, you need a wild rice blend—the kind that has brown rice, wild rice, red rice, black rice, and so on in it. This is great as an accompaniment to holiday dinners, but is also fantastic as a stuffing for acorn squash or other winter squashes.

ACTIVE TIME	FUNCTION	RELEASE	TOTAL TIME
5 minutes	Manual (High)	Natural + Quick	1 hour

Egg-Free, Nut-Free, Dairy-Free, Gluten-Free, Vegan • 10 Ingredients or Less • SERVES 6

1 cup wild rice blend

1 cup frozen mirepoix or ⅓ cup each diced onion, carrot, and celery

1 tablespoon vegetable oil

2 teaspoons poultry seasoning

1 teaspoon kosher salt

1 cup water

Toasted almonds, dried cranberries, and/or golden raisins, for serving (optional)

1. In the Instant Pot, combine the rice, mirepoix, oil, poultry seasoning, salt, and water. Stir to combine.

2. Secure the lid on the pot. Close the pressure-release valve. Select MANUAL and set the pot at HIGH pressure for 25 minutes. At the end of the cooking time, allow the pot to sit undisturbed for 20 minutes, then quick-release any remaining pressure.

3. Transfer to a serving bowl or platter. Top with almonds, cranberries, and/or raisins, if desired, and serve.

Simple Wild Rice Pilaf (page 185)

Cilantro-Lime Millet Pilaf

Millet is more than just birdseed! In many parts of Asia and Africa, it is a staple part of the diet. It's inexpensive and relatively high in fiber and B-complex vitamins. It's a chewy, nutty grain that is a wonderful, gluten-free addition to your meals.

ACTIVE TIME	FUNCTION	RELEASE	TOTAL TIME
10 minutes	Manual (High)	Natural + Quick	40 minutes

Egg-Free, Nut-Free, Dairy-Free, Gluten-Free, Vegan • 10 Ingredients or Less • SERVES 4

1 cup chopped green onions

1 cup millet

1 teaspoon kosher salt

1 tablespoon olive oil

1 cup water

1 cup chopped fresh cilantro or parsley

Zest and juice of 1 lime

1. In the Instant Pot, combine the green onions, millet, salt, olive oil, and water.

2. Secure the lid on the pot. Close the pressure-release valve. Select MANUAL and set the pot at HIGH pressure for 10 minutes. At the end of the cooking time, allow the pot to sit undisturbed for 10 minutes, then quick-release any remaining pressure.

3. Stir in the cilantro and lime zest and juice and serve.

Cinnamon-Spiced Bulgur Pilaf with Red Lentils

This is a great base recipe that you can use with a variety of different seasonings to mix and match with your main dishes. Be sure to use whole-grain bulgur—not quick-soaking bulgur—for this dish.

ACTIVE TIME	FUNCTION	RELEASE	TOTAL TIME
10 minutes	Sauté (Normal); Manual (High)	Natural + Quick	35 minutes

Egg-Free, Nut-Free, Dairy-Free, Vegan • 10 Ingredients or Less • SERVES 6

2 tablespoons vegetable oil

1 large onion, thinly sliced

1½ teaspoons kosher salt

½ teaspoon ground cinnamon

½ teaspoon ground allspice

1¾ cups water

1 cup whole-grain red wheat bulgur

½ cup dried red lentils

¼ cup chopped fresh parsley

Toasted pine nuts (optional)

1. Select SAUTÉ/NORMAL on the Instant Pot. When the pot is hot, add the oil. Once the oil is hot, add the onion and salt. Cook, stirring occasionally, until the onion is browned, about 5 minutes.

2. Stir in the cinnamon and allspice and cook for 30 seconds.

3. Add ¼ cup of the water to deglaze the pot, scraping up the browned bits. Add the bulgur, lentils, and remaining 1½ cups of the water. Select CANCEL.

4. Secure the lid on the pot. Close the pressure-release valve. Select MANUAL and set the pot at HIGH pressure for 5 minutes. At the end of the cooking time, allow the pot to sit undisturbed for 10 minutes, then quick-release any remaining pressure.

5. Stir gently to fluff up the bulgur. Stir in the parsley and pine nuts, if using, and serve.

Mushroom-Barley Pilaf

I used to make a similar dish almost thirty years ago. Why I stopped making it, I don't know, but I'm glad I have a pressure cooker for this dish, because it sure cuts down on the time, the babysitting, and the cooking water frothing all over the stove when I forgot about it. This dish is great eaten hot as a side dish with vegetables, or cold, mixed with chopped cucumbers, onions, and tomatoes as a salad.

ACTIVE TIME	FUNCTION	RELEASE	TOTAL TIME
10 minutes	Sauté (Normal); Manual (High)	Natural + Quick	45 minutes

Egg-Free, Nut-Free, Dairy-Free, Vegan • 10 Ingredients or Less • SERVES 6

2 tablespoons butter or vegetable oil

½ cup diced onion

2 cups chopped button or cremini mushrooms

1 cup pearled barley

1 teaspoon kosher salt

1 teaspoon black pepper

1 cup water

1 to 2 tablespoons red wine vinegar or fresh lemon juice

¼ cup chopped fresh parsley

1. Select SAUTÉ/NORMAL on the Instant Pot. When the pot is hot, add the butter. Once the butter is melted, add the onion and stir for about 30 seconds. Add the mushrooms and stir to coat. Add the barley, salt, pepper, and water. Select CANCEL.

2. Secure the lid on the pot. Close the pressure-release valve. Select MANUAL and set the pot at HIGH pressure for 15 minutes. At the end of the cooking time, allow the pot to sit undisturbed for 10 minutes, then quick-release any remaining pressure.

3. Stir in the vinegar and parsley and serve.

Couscous Pilaf with Feta and Red Onion

Don't skip the feta and red onion in this dish—they really make all the difference in providing a great combination of flavors. If you are dairy-free, you can use extra lemon juice rather than the feta to add a little tang at the end.

ACTIVE TIME	FUNCTION	RELEASE	TOTAL TIME
5 minutes	Sauté (Normal); Manual (High)	Natural + Quick	25 minutes

Egg-Free, Nut-Free • 10 Ingredients or Less • SERVES 4

2 tablespoons vegetable oil

1 teaspoon cumin seeds

1 teaspoon ground turmeric

1 cup frozen peas and carrots

1 cup Israeli couscous

½ cup diced yellow onion

1 teaspoon kosher salt

1 teaspoon garam masala

1 cup water

½ cup chopped red onion

½ cup crumbled feta cheese

Black pepper

1. Select SAUTÉ/NORMAL on the Instant Pot. When the pot is hot, add the oil. Once the oil is hot, stir in the cumin seeds and turmeric; allow them to sizzle for 10 seconds. Select CANCEL.

2. Add the peas and carrots, couscous, yellow onion, salt, garam masala, and water. Stir to combine.

3. Secure the lid on the pot. Close the pressure-release valve. Select MANUAL and set the pot at HIGH pressure for 3 minutes. At the end of the cooking time, allow the pot to sit undisturbed for 5 minutes, then quick-release any remaining pressure.

4. Stir in the red onion and feta cheese, sprinkle with pepper, and serve.

EGGS & CHEESE

Egg Loaf

I know this sounds like an insane method to make eggs, but it's actually #ruthlessefficiency at work. I first made this egg loaf two years ago and use it often if I'm making eggs for egg salads. The egg cooks up evenly (no need to worry about dark yolks!), it chops up easily, and it looks very pretty when it's done.

ACTIVE TIME	FUNCTION	RELEASE	TOTAL TIME
5 minutes	Manual (High)	Quick	20 minutes

Nut-Free, Dairy-Free, Gluten-Free, Low-Carb • 10 Ingredients or Less • SERVES 8

Vegetable oil

6 large eggs

Melted butter (optional)

Kosher salt (optional)

Black pepper (optional)

1. Generously grease a 6×3-inch round baking pan with oil. Carefully crack the eggs into the pan, taking care not to break the yolks. Cover the pan with foil.

2. Pour 1½ cups water into the Instant Pot. Place a trivet in the pot. Place the pan on the trivet.

3. Secure the lid on the pot. Close the pressure-release valve. Select MANUAL and set the pot at HIGH pressure for 4 minutes. At the end of the cooking time, use a quick release to depressurize.

4. Run a knife around the edge of the pan to loosen the egg loaf and turn it out onto a plate. Dice the loaf and use it for egg salad or mix with melted butter and salt and pepper to taste for the best snack you've never had.

Egg Cups

These cups are cute and portable, making for an easy breakfast to take to work. They're also highly customizable, so each family member can decide what they want in their egg cups.

ACTIVE TIME	FUNCTION	RELEASE	TOTAL TIME
10 minutes	Manual (High)	Quick	35 minutes

Nut-Free, Gluten-Free, Low-Carb • 10 Ingredients or Less • SERVES 4

4 large eggs

½ cup cottage cheese

¼ cup heavy cream

¼ cup shredded cheddar cheese

1 teaspoon kosher salt

1 teaspoon black pepper

2 dashes hot sauce (optional)

½ cup diced vegetables, such as onion, bell pepper, or tomato

¼ cup chopped fresh cilantro or parsley

1. In a blender, combine the eggs, cottage cheese, cream, cheddar cheese, salt, pepper, and hot sauce, if using. Blend on low speed until well combined. Stir in the vegetables and cilantro.

2. Divide the mixture among four 4-ounce glass jars with lids, ramekins, or silicone baby food containers. Set the lids on the jars but do not tighten (cover ramekins or silicone baby food containers loosely with foil).

3. Pour 1½ cups water into the Instant Pot. Place a trivet in the pot. Set the jars on the trivet.

4. Secure the lid on the pot. Close the pressure-release valve. Select MANUAL and set the pot at HIGH pressure for 5 minutes. At the end of the cooking time, use a quick release to depressurize.

5. Carefully remove the hot jars from the trivet and allow to cool for 15 minutes. Tighten the lids (but not too tight). Store in the refrigerator for up to 4 days. To reheat, microwave on high for 30 seconds (remove any foil covering before microwaving).

**Italian Greens
and Eggs** (page 200)

Italian Greens and Eggs

This is a super-efficient recipe that allows you to make eggs and veggies at the same time. It's a light and colorful supper, and if you make more eggs than the recipe calls for, you will have breakfast done at the same time. How's that for #ruthlessefficiency?

ACTIVE TIME	FUNCTION	RELEASE	TOTAL TIME
10 minutes	Manual (High)	Natural + Quick	35 minutes

Nut-Free, Gluten-Free, Low-Carb • 10 Ingredients or Less • SERVES 4

1 cup thinly sliced onion

1 teaspoon kosher salt

1 teaspoon black pepper

¼ cup water

1 (16-ounce) package frozen chopped kale, broken into 3 or 4 blocks

1 red bell pepper, stemmed, seeded, and sliced

4 large eggs

4 ounces grated Parmesan cheese

1 teaspoon ground nutmeg

Cooked rice or bread, for serving

1. In the Instant Pot, combine the onion, salt, pepper, and water. Stir to combine.

2. Place the kale on top of the onion. Scatter the bell pepper on top of the kale. Do not stir. Place a trivet on top of the vegetables. Place the eggs (still in their shells) on top of the trivet.

3. Secure the lid on the pot. Close the pressure-release valve. Select MANUAL and set the pot at HIGH pressure for 5 minutes. At the end of the cooking time, allow the pot to sit undisturbed for 5 minutes, then quick-release any remaining pressure.

4. Meanwhile, fill a large bowl with ice cubes and water. Remove the eggs and place in the ice bath. Allow to cool for 5 minutes.

5. Add the Parmesan cheese and nutmeg to the hot vegetables and stir until well blended.

6. Peel and slice the hard-cooked eggs and gently mix them into the vegetables. Serve with rice or bread.

Homemade Paneer

Paneer is a creamy, homemade cheese that is a great addition to various dishes. DO NOT USE ULTRA-HIGH PASTEURIZED (UHT) DAIRY. DO NOT USE DAIRY WITH CARRAGEENAN ADDED. Yes, I know I'm yelling, but I cannot emphasize this enough. These milks will just not separate as they should. At all. If you open up the Instant Pot and your paneer hasn't separated, your milk had some kind of personal issues. In this case, try putting the pot on Sauté and cooking it some more. You may need to add some more vinegar, too. If your paneer is crumbly, it's a sign you didn't press it with a heavy enough weight, or for long enough. If in doubt, place two or three cans on top of it so it compresses beautifully.

ACTIVE TIME	FUNCTION	RELEASE	TOTAL TIME
20 minutes	Manual (Low)	Natural + Quick	45 minutes plus 2 hours draining time

Egg-Free, Nut-Free, Gluten-Free, Low-Carb • 10 Ingredients or Less • SERVES 4

1 quart half-and-half

¼ cup white vinegar

1. In the Instant Pot, combine the half-and-half and vinegar.

2. Secure the lid on the pot. Close the pressure-release valve. Select MANUAL and set the pot at LOW pressure for 4 minutes. At the end of the cooking time, allow the pot to sit undisturbed for 10 minutes, then quick-release any remaining pressure.

3. When you open the pot, the half-and-half will have separated into curds and a watery whey. Stir well. Line a fine-mesh strainer with cheesecloth. Place the strainer over a bowl and pour the mixture through cheesecloth; discard the whey.

4. Gather up the cheesecloth tightly around the curds. Place a heavy weight on them to help the whey drain and the curds form a cohesive block or ball. (I use a plain plastic tofu mold to form a nice square block and weigh it down with a can of beans, but you can let it be a flattened round ball instead.) Let the curds drain for 2 hours. (They do not need to be refrigerated while draining). Refrigerate if using within 1 to 2 days, or freeze for up to 3 months if not using right away.

Broccoli and Cheese Frittata

This recipe was tested with a metal pan and a relatively low trivet. If you use glass or silicone, or a high trivet, you will need to increase cooking times. I also use frozen broccoli since it tends to be softer than raw broccoli and usually is chopped finely and consistently, which makes cooking this frittata super fast.

ACTIVE TIME	FUNCTION	RELEASE	TOTAL TIME
10 minutes	Manual (High)	Natural + Quick	55 minutes

Nut-Free, Gluten-Free, Low-Carb • 10 Ingredients or Less • SERVES 4

Vegetable oil

1 cup stemmed, seeded, and sliced red, yellow, or orange bell pepper

2 cups frozen chopped broccoli

4 large eggs

1 cup half-and-half

1 teaspoon kosher salt

1 teaspoon black pepper

1 cup shredded cheddar cheese

1. Generously grease a 6×3-inch round baking pan with oil; set aside.

2. Arrange the bell pepper in the bottom of the pan. Scatter the broccoli on top of the peppers.

3. In a medium bowl, whisk together the eggs, half-and-half, salt, and pepper. Stir in ¾ cup of the shredded cheese.

4. Pour the egg mixture over the vegetables and cover the pan with foil.

5. Pour 1½ cups water into the Instant Pot. Place a trivet in the pot. Set the pan on the trivet.

6. Secure the lid on the pot. Close the pressure-release valve. Select MANUAL and set the pot at HIGH pressure for 25 minutes. At the end of the cooking time, allow the pot to sit undisturbed for 10 minutes, then quick-release any remaining pressure. Meanwhile, preheat the broiler.

7. Let the frittata stand for 5 minutes. Using a knife, gently loosen the sides of the frittata and turn it out onto a baking sheet.

8. Sprinkle the top of the frittata with the remaining ¼ cup cheese and broil for 2 to 3 minutes, or until the cheese is melted.

9. Slice into wedges and serve.

Asparagus Gribiche

Gri-who?? *Gribiche*. Another word for fat-bomb deliciousness that can be used on top of anything you please. The asparagus is done al dente with this method, but if you like yours a little more done, give it an additional minute under pressure.

ACTIVE TIME	FUNCTION	RELEASE	TOTAL TIME
10 minutes	Manual (High)	Natural + Quick	25 minutes

Nut-Free, Dairy-Free, Gluten-Free, Low-Carb • 10 Ingredients or Less • SERVES 4

2 large eggs

1 pound asparagus, trimmed and cut into 1-inch pieces

1 tablespoon Dijon mustard

¼ cup vegetable oil

1 tablespoon apple cider vinegar

2 to 3 tablespoons chopped dill pickle

1 tablespoon chopped fresh parsley

1 teaspoon granulated sugar

½ teaspoon kosher salt

½ teaspoon black pepper

1. Pour 1½ cups water into the Instant Pot. Place a trivet in the pot. Place the eggs (still in their shells) on one side of the trivet.

2. Tightly wrap the asparagus in foil and place on the trivet next to the eggs.

3. Secure the lid on the pot. Close the pressure-release valve. Select MANUAL and set the pot at HIGH pressure for 5 minutes. At the end of the cooking time, allow the pot to sit undisturbed for 5 minutes, then quick-release any remaining pressure. Meanwhile, fill a medium bowl with ice cubes and water.

4. Remove the eggs and place them in the ice water bath for 5 minutes. Peel and finely dice the eggs.

5. In a small bowl, combine the mustard, oil, vinegar, pickle, parsley, sugar, salt, and pepper. Stir in the chopped eggs.

6. Place the asparagus on a serving platter and spoon the gribiche on top. Serve.

Spinach and Cheese Strata

I call this a strata, but it really doesn't have layers in it. I just mixed everything up and it tasted fine! Less effort, same taste? Sign me up! You can prepare this mixture the night before and refrigerate it until you're ready to cook.

ACTIVE TIME	FUNCTION	RELEASE	TOTAL TIME
15 minutes	Manual (High)	Natural + Quick	50 minutes

Nut-Free • 10 Ingredients or Less • SERVES 4

Vegetable oil

6 large eggs

1 cup half-and-half

1 teaspoon kosher salt

1 teaspoon black pepper

4 slices sourdough bread, cut into cubes

3 cups chopped fresh spinach

1 cup chopped green onions

1 cup shredded Swiss cheese

1. Generously grease a 6×3-inch springform pan with oil and line the bottom with a circle of parchment paper. Set aside.

2. In a large mixing bowl, whisk together the eggs, half-and-half, salt, and pepper. Stir in the bread cubes, spinach, green onions, and Swiss cheese. Pour the mixture into the prepared pan.

3. Pour 1½ cups water into the Instant Pot. Place a trivet in the pot. Place the pan with the bread mixture on the trivet.

4. Secure the lid on the pot. Close the pressure-release valve. Select MANUAL and set the pot at HIGH pressure for 15 minutes. At the end of the cooking time, allow the pot to sit undisturbed for 10 minutes, then quick-release any remaining pressure.

5. Carefully remove the pan from the trivet. Check the center of the strata to ensure that it is cooked through. If needed, pat the top dry with a paper towel.

6. Let stand for 5 minutes before releasing the springform pan ring and removing it.

7. Slice into wedges and serve.

DESSERTS & DRINKS

Hot Fudge Pudding Cake

I know this sounds utterly weird, but #trustUrvashi, because it works. Once you pour the hot water on top, do not stir it. The water will mix with the cocoa you sprinkled on top to make a lovely chocolate sauce. Once the cake cools, the sauce gets absorbed into the cake, so you may want to eat this while it's hot—with a dollop of vanilla ice cream on top, because ice cream!

ACTIVE TIME	FUNCTION	RELEASE	TOTAL TIME
15 minutes	Manual (High)	Natural + Quick	55 minutes

Nut-Free • 10 Ingredients or Less • SERVES 6

½ cup (1 stick) unsalted butter, melted, plus room-temperature butter for greasing the pan

¾ cup all-purpose flour

1¼ cups packed dark brown sugar

½ cup whole milk

½ cup unsweetened cocoa powder

2 large eggs

2 teaspoons baking powder

1 teaspoon vanilla extract

1¼ cups boiling water

Ice cream or sweetened whipped cream, for serving (optional)

1. Grease a 6×3-inch round baking pan with softened butter; set aside.

2. In a large mixing bowl, combine the melted butter, flour, ¾ cup of the brown sugar, milk, ¼ cup of the cocoa, eggs, baking powder, and vanilla. Using a hand mixer, beat until smooth. Pour the batter into the pan and sprinkle with the remaining ½ cup brown sugar and ¼ cup cocoa powder.

3. Pour 1½ cups water into the Instant Pot. Place a trivet in the pot. Place the pan on the trivet. Carefully pour the boiling water on top of the batter. Do not stir.

4. Secure the lid on the pot. Close the pressure-release valve. Select MANUAL and set the pot at HIGH pressure for 20 minutes. At the end of the cooking time, allow the pot to sit undisturbed for 10 minutes, then quick-release any remaining pressure.

5. Serve warm with ice cream or whipped cream, if desired.

Box Mix Blueberry Cake

I almost never use box mixes. But every once in a while, it's a fun treat. Be sure to use a 7-ounce package of muffin mix, not a full-size box. That way you can have a quick, small cake that feeds four without worrying about excess leftovers endlessly calling your name.

ACTIVE TIME	FUNCTION	RELEASE	TOTAL TIME
10 minutes	Manual (High)	Natural	1 hour 5 minutes

Nut-Free • 10 Ingredients or Less • SERVES 4

Vegetable oil

1 cup blueberries

1 tablespoon granulated sugar, plus more for sprinkling

½ teaspoon ground nutmeg

1 (7-ounce) package blueberry muffin mix

½ cup whole milk

1. Lightly grease a 6×3-inch round baking pan with oil; set aside.

2. In a small bowl, toss together the blueberries, sugar, and nutmeg. Spread the mixture over the bottom of the pan.

3. Prepare the muffin mix according to the package directions, using the ½ cup milk for the liquid. Spread the batter on top of the blueberries; cover the pan with foil.

4. Pour 2 cups water into the Instant Pot. Place a trivet in the pot. Place the pan on the trivet.

5. Secure the lid on the pot. Close the pressure-release valve. Select MANUAL and set the pot at HIGH pressure for 35 minutes. At the end of the cooking time, use a natural release to depressurize.

6. Preheat the broiler. Transfer the cake to a wire rack. Remove the foil. Let the cake cool for 5 to 10 minutes. Loosen the sides of the cake and invert onto a broiler-safe pan.

7. Sprinkle the cake with a little sugar; broil until the sugar is melted and caramelized, 5 to 7 minutes.

8. Let cool slightly before serving.

NOTE: Some brands of muffin mix contain animal shortening (lard). Read the label to be sure the mix you buy is vegetarian.

Steamed Sponge Cake

This light, steamed sponge cake is sort of like what you would see on dim sum menus. It's very lightly sweetened, so feel free to add more sugar if you prefer. Oh, and if you've never tried pandan extract? Remedy that immediately! If you search my TwoSleevers website for "pandan," you will find many other recipes that use the delectable flavoring.

ACTIVE TIME	FUNCTION	RELEASE	TOTAL TIME
15 minutes	Manual (High)	Natural + Quick	55 minutes plus 30 minutes cooling time

Nut-Free, Dairy-Free · 10 Ingredients or Less · SERVES 4

¼ cup vegetable oil, plus more for greasing the pan

4 large eggs

¾ cup granulated sugar

½ cup full-fat coconut milk or evaporated milk

½ teaspoon pandan or vanilla extract (see Note)

1¼ cups all-purpose flour

2 teaspoons baking powder

Variations

Substitute ½ teaspoon lemon, orange, or almond extract for the pandan extract.

1. Grease a 6-cup Bundt pan with oil; set aside.

2. Using a hand mixer, blend the oil, eggs, and sugar until the sugar dissolves and the eggs are frothy. Add the evaporated milk and extract and continue blending. Add the flour and baking powder. Beat on low speed until the batter is smooth. Pour the batter into the pan and cover with foil.

3. Pour 1½ cups water into the Instant Pot. Place a trivet in the pot. Place the pan on the trivet.

4. Secure the lid on the pot. Close the pressure-release valve. Select MANUAL and set the pot at HIGH pressure for 20 minutes. At the end of the cooking time, allow the pot to sit undisturbed for 10 minutes, then quick-release any remaining pressure.

5. Carefully remove the pan from the pot. Let the cake cool in the pan on a wire rack for 10 minutes. Release the springform pan ring and remove it. Allow the cake to cool completely before serving, about 20 minutes.

NOTE: Pandan extract is used in Southeast Asian, Indian, and Indonesian cooking. It has a lightly floral, basmati rice–like fragrance and taste, and a bright green color. Look for it at Asian markets or online.

Mango Cheesecake

I used frozen mangoes for this dish so that everyone could find them easily, but also so that you wouldn't use green mangoes and then write to me about how horrible my recipe was—which has happened with other mango recipes I've shared! This is a deliciously creamy and slightly tangy cheesecake that feels utterly indulgent. I've made the crust with gingersnaps, pistachios, and graham crackers—all three versions were wonderful, so feel free to use whichever you prefer.

ACTIVE TIME	FUNCTION	RELEASE	TOTAL TIME
45 minutes	Manual (High)	Natural + Quick	1 hour 50 minutes plus 4 hours chilling time

Nut-Free, Gluten-Free • SERVES 8

For the Crust

Cooking spray

1¼ cups gingersnap or graham cracker crumbs or ground pistachios

3 tablespoons unsalted butter, melted

For the Filling

2 cups mango chunks (thawed if frozen)

2 tablespoons fresh lemon juice

2 (8-ounce) packages cream cheese, softened

½ teaspoon ground cardamom

4 or 5 saffron threads

½ cup granulated sugar

3 large eggs

(ingredients continued)

1. **For the crust:** Lightly spray a 7×3-inch springform pan with cooking spray. Line the bottom of the pan with a circle of parchment paper.

2. In a small bowl, mix together the crumbs and butter. Pat the mixture firmly into the bottom and about 1 inch up the sides of the pan. Place the pan in the freezer to allow the crust to set while you make the filling.

3. **For the filling:** In a blender or food processor, combine the mango chunks, lemon juice, cream cheese, cardamom, saffron, and sugar. Blend until smooth, scraping down the sides as needed. Add the eggs and blend until well incorporated and pourable, 10 to 15 seconds. Pour the mixture into the crust and cover with foil.

4. Pour 1½ cups water into the Instant Pot. Place a trivet with handles in the pot, making sure the handles are in an upright position. Place the pan on the trivet. (If you do not have a trivet with handles, make a sling with foil and place it under the pan so you can easily lift it out of the pot.)

5. Secure the lid on the pot. Close the pressure-release valve. Select MANUAL and set the pot at HIGH pressure for 55 minutes. At the end of the cooking time, allow the pot to sit undisturbed for 10 minutes, then quick-release any remaining pressure. (The sides of the cheesecake

(continued)

For the Topping

2 tablespoons sour cream

½ cup mango purée (see Note)

2 teaspoons sugar

1 ripe mango, peeled and sliced (optional)

will be set, but the middle will still have a little jiggle. This will set as the cheesecake cools.) Use the handles on the trivet to carefully lift the pan out of the pot. Cool the cheesecake on a wire rack for 1 hour.

6. For the topping: In a medium bowl, stir together the sour cream, mango purée, and sugar. Spread the topping over the cheesecake.

7. Chill in the refrigerator for at least 4 hours or overnight.

8. Top the cheesecake with mango slices, if desired, and serve.

NOTE: To get ½ cup mango purée, blend ¾ cup thawed frozen mango chunks with 1 teaspoon water in a blender or food processor until smooth.

Coconut Rice Pudding with Saffron, Raisins, and Cashews

I like the slight hint of coconut and the creaminess of the Arborio rice in this dish. Sometimes I add canned pineapple to the cooled pudding, or cooked apples with a little apple pie spice instead of the cardamom. Make this once as written and then let your imagination go wild with different flavor combinations.

ACTIVE TIME	FUNCTION	RELEASE	TOTAL TIME
10 minutes	Manual (High)	Natural + Quick	50 minutes

Egg-Free, Gluten-Free • 10 Ingredients or Less • SERVES 4

¾ cup Arborio rice, rinsed and drained

1 (13.5-ounce) can full-fat coconut milk

5 ounces evaporated milk

½ cup granulated sugar

½ cup raisins

½ cup cashews

¼ teaspoon ground cardamom

3 or 4 saffron threads

½ cup water

1. In the Instant Pot, combine the rice, half the coconut milk, the evaporated milk, sugar, raisins, cashews, cardamom, saffron, and water.

2. Secure the lid on the pot. Close the pressure-release valve. Select MANUAL and set the pot at HIGH pressure for 20 minutes. At the end of the cooking time, allow the pot to sit undisturbed for 10 minutes, then quick-release any remaining pressure.

3. When you open the lid, there will be a little bit of curdling—don't worry about this. Stir to reincorporate all the ingredients. Add the remaining coconut milk and stir to combine.

4. Serve warm or chilled.

Eight Treasures Rice Soup

I really dislike buying ingredients that only get used for one dish in a cookbook. So this recipe is one where you can use the millet, barley, and adzuki beans you bought for other recipes in this book. It's also a comforting, slightly sweet dessert. Some versions of this dish tend to be soupy, others tend to be sticky. Mine is on the soupy side. (If you would like it to be thicker, let it stand for 5 to 10 minutes after the pressure has been released before serving.) Other versions include jujube, red palm sugar, and lotus seeds, but since many of us don't have easy access to them, I substituted other ingredients for those.

ACTIVE TIME	FUNCTION	RELEASE	TOTAL TIME
10 minutes	Manual (High)	Natural + Quick	50 minutes

Egg-Free, Dairy-Free, Vegan • 10 Ingredients or Less • SERVES 4

⅓ cup glutinous white rice, rinsed and drained

¼ cup dried red adzuki beans, soaked and drained (see page 108)

¼ cup granulated sugar

2 tablespoons raisins

2 tablespoons black rice, rinsed and drained

2 tablespoons millet

2 tablespoons barley

2 tablespoons dried mung beans

2 tablespoons peanuts

4 cups water

1. In the Instant Pot, combine the white rice, adzuki beans, sugar, raisins, black rice, millet, barley, mung beans, peanuts, and water.

2. Secure the lid on the pot. Close the pressure-release valve. Select MANUAL and set the pot at HIGH pressure for 25 minutes. At the end of the cooking time, allow the pot to sit undisturbed for 15 minutes, then quick-release any remaining pressure.

3. Stir well before serving.

Sweet Red Bean Soup

Most of us aren't used to having beans in our dessert, but it is a good way to get some nutrition—not to mention to have an easy, tasty dish at the end of it all. This recipe uses adzuki beans, which are also called for in Simple Adzuki Beans and Sticky Rice (page 148) and Eight Treasures Rice Soup (page 219), so if you buy a bag, you'll have more than one way to use them.

ACTIVE TIME	FUNCTION	RELEASE	TOTAL TIME
10 minutes	Manual (High); Sauté (Normal)	Natural + Quick	1 hour 5 minutes

Egg-Free, Nut-Free, Dairy-Free, Gluten-Free, Vegan • 10 Ingredients or Less • SERVES 8

1 cup dried adzuki beans, soaked and drained (see page 108)

½ cup black rice, rinsed and drained

¼ cup tangerine zest (from 2 tangerines) or orange zest (from 1 large orange)

½ cup granulated sugar

5 cups water

½ cup coconut cream or 1 cup full-fat coconut milk

1. In the Instant Pot, combine the adzuki beans, rice, tangerine zest, sugar, and water.

2. Secure the lid on the pot. Close the pressure-release valve. Select MANUAL and set the pot at HIGH pressure for 40 minutes. At the end of the cooking time, allow the pot to sit undisturbed for 15 minutes, then quick-release any remaining pressure.

3. Using an immersion blender, purée some of the soup to thicken it slightly, 20 to 25 seconds, leaving some whole beans.

4. If necessary, select SAUTÉ/NORMAL and cook the soup until thickened and slowly bubbling, 5 to 10 minutes. (You want the bubbles to be dark, syrupy, and thick-looking.)

5. Stir in the coconut cream and serve.

Mixed Fruit Kesari

This dish is referred to as a halva through much of India, but when I use that term here, people expect something made from sesame or nuts. So I use the South Indian word *kesari* to describe it. Kesari also means "orange," and the few little saffron threads you use here add both fragrance and color.

ACTIVE TIME	FUNCTION	RELEASE	TOTAL TIME
10 minutes	Manual (High)	Natural + Quick	35 minutes

Egg-Free, Nut-Free, Dairy-Free, Vegan • 10 Ingredients or Less • SERVES 4

½ cup farina (such as Cream of Wheat)

⅓ cup chopped mixed dried fruit

¼ cup granulated sugar

¼ cup Ghee (page 240) or vegetable oil

1 teaspoon ground cardamom

3 or 4 saffron threads, crushed

¾ cup water

Heavy cream and/or milk, for serving (optional)

1. In a 6×3-inch round baking pan, mix together the farina, dried fruit, sugar, ghee, cardamom, saffron, and water.

2. Pour 1½ cups water into the Instant Pot. Place a trivet in the pot. Place the pan on the trivet.

3. Secure the lid on the pot. Close the pressure-release valve. Select MANUAL and set the pot at HIGH pressure for 10 minutes. At the end of the cooking time, allow the pot to sit undisturbed for 5 minutes, then quick-release any remaining pressure.

4. Carefully remove the pan and stir the mixture until smooth.

5. Serve hot or chilled. If desired, stir in some cream and/or milk for a porridge-like texture.

Apple-Quinoa Porridge

Think of this recipe as a starting point for a variety of different fruit and flavor combinations to make your morning porridge something to look forward to. Be sure to rinse the quinoa ahead of time to get rid of any bitterness.

ACTIVE TIME	FUNCTION	RELEASE	TOTAL TIME
10 minutes	Manual (High)	Quick	20 minutes

Egg-Free, Nut-Free, Gluten-Free • 10 Ingredients or Less • SERVES 6

1 cup quinoa, rinsed and drained

1 cup water

1 cup peeled diced apples

1 (12-ounce) can evaporated milk

1 cup sweetened condensed milk

1 teaspoon apple pie spice

¼ cup chopped walnuts (optional)

1. In the Instant Pot, combine the quinoa and water; stir to combine. Scatter the apples over the top (do not stir).

2. Secure the lid on the pot. Close the pressure-release valve. Select MANUAL and set the pot at HIGH pressure for 1 minute. At the end of the cooking time, use a quick release to depressurize.

3. Stir in the evaporated milk, condensed milk, and apple pie spice.

4. Add the walnuts, if using. Serve hot immediately or chill and serve. (If you chill it, the porridge may thicken and you may need to add a little milk just before serving.)

NOTE: If you are using the nuts, you can either add them just as they are or sauté them in a pan with a little butter or Ghee (page 240) before adding to the finished porridge.

Boston Brown Bread

I used a Bundt pan rather than the traditional coffee can, and I skipped a few different flours, but this simple bread recipe makes a great accompaniment to Boston Baked Beans (page 147) or any other beans in this book. Slightly sweet, moist, and hearty, you can make this bread at the same time as the Boston Baked Beans. Just put the ingredients for the beans in the Instant Pot. Place a trivet in the pot, place the covered bread pan on the trivet, and cook them both for 40 minutes instead of 30, and you'll have a two-for-one dish.

ACTIVE TIME	FUNCTION	RELEASE	TOTAL TIME
15 minutes	Manual (High)	Natural	1 hour 10 minutes

Nut-Free • 10 Ingredients or Less • SERVES 8

1 tablespoon vegetable oil, plus more for greasing the pan

1 large egg

1 cup buttermilk (see Note)

¼ cup molasses

¼ cup granulated sugar

1½ cups whole wheat flour

½ cup cornmeal

½ cup chopped walnuts

¼ cup raisins

2 teaspoons baking powder

1 teaspoon ground allspice

1. Generously grease a 6-cup Bundt pan with oil; set aside.

2. In a large mixing bowl, whisk together the oil, egg, buttermilk, molasses, and sugar.

3. Stir in the flour, cornmeal, walnuts, raisins, baking powder, and allspice. Pour the batter into the pan and cover with foil.

4. Pour 1½ cups water into the pot. Place a trivet in the pot. Place the pan on the trivet.

5. Secure the lid on the pot. Close the pressure-release valve. Select MANUAL and set the pot at HIGH pressure for 30 minutes. At the end of the cooking time, use a natural release to depressurize.

6. Carefully remove the cake from the pot. Allow the cake to cool in the pan for 10 minutes. Run a knife around the edge of the pan, then unmold the cake onto a serving plate.

NOTE: If you don't have buttermilk, combine 1 cup whole milk with 1 tablespoon apple cider or white wine vinegar; let stand for about 10 minutes, then use in the recipe in place of the buttermilk.

Chess Pie Custard

If you've ever had a proper Southern chess pie, you may remember the super-sweet goodness of that delight. I used that as inspiration, but my version doesn't heat up your kitchen, doesn't have a crust, and uses a lot less sugar. This way you can tell yourself this is a healthy version.

ACTIVE TIME	FUNCTION	RELEASE	TOTAL TIME
10 minutes	Manual (High)	Natural + Quick	1 hour 5 minutes

Nut-Free, Gluten-Free • 10 Ingredients or Less • SERVES 6

½ cup (1 stick) unsalted butter, melted, plus room-temperature butter for greasing the pan

½ cup granulated sugar

4 large eggs

⅓ cup evaporated milk

2 tablespoons cornmeal

1 tablespoon white vinegar

2 teaspoons vanilla extract

1. Grease a 7×3-inch round baking pan with softened butter; set aside.

2. In a large bowl, whisk together the melted butter and sugar until the sugar is mostly dissolved.

3. Whisk in the eggs, evaporated milk, cornmeal, vinegar, and vanilla. Pour the mixture into the pan and cover with foil.

4. Pour 1½ cups water into the Instant Pot. Place a trivet in the pot. Set the pan on the trivet.

5. Secure the lid on the pot. Close the pressure-release valve. Select MANUAL and set the pot at HIGH pressure for 20 minutes. At the end of the cooking time, allow the pot to sit undisturbed for 10 minutes, then quick-release any remaining pressure.

6. Cool the custard on a wire rack for about 15 minutes. Serve warm or transfer to the refrigerator to cool completely, then serve chilled.

Cardamom Yogurt

For those of you who want to make yogurt in the Instant Pot, this is a good starter recipe. The gelatin really helps it set, but you must let it sit in the fridge overnight (and be sure to use a vegetarian gelatin). Even if you are a yogurt pro, you might like the smoother texture of this yogurt. You will note that I haven't used the first Yogurt cycle on the Instant Pot. I have tested it both ways, and I don't find there is a difference in texture from heating to 180°F versus heating to body temperature, and this is faster.

ACTIVE TIME	FUNCTION	RELEASE	TOTAL TIME
20 minutes	Yogurt	Natural	14 hours plus 20 minutes

Egg-Free, Nut-Free, Gluten-Free · 10 Ingredients or Less · Makes 6 cups

2 cups whole milk

½ cup heavy whipping cream

1½ teaspoons unflavored vegetarian gelatin

3 tablespoons Greek yogurt

½ teaspoon ground cardamom, ground cinnamon, or apple pie spice

¼ cup granulated sugar

1½ teaspoons honey (optional)

1. In a medium microwave-safe bowl, combine the milk and cream and heat on high in the microwave for 2 minutes.

2. In a small bowl, combine ½ cup of the warm milk mixture and the gelatin. Stir until smooth, then add back to the rest of the milk mixture. Transfer to the Instant Pot.

3. Add the yogurt and cardamom and stir until well combined.

4. Secure the lid on the Instant Pot. Select YOGURT (the timer will show 8 hours by default). At the end of the incubation time, stir in the sugar and honey, if using. (Don't add the sweeteners before the yogurt is set, as they can interfere with setting.)

5. Chill for at least 6 hours to allow the yogurt to firm up before serving. Cover and store in the refrigerator for up to one week.

Caramel Custard

In this recipe, the Instant Pot is being used as a self-contained steamer—not as a pressure cooker. So you need to leave the pressure valve set to Venting when cooking the custard. Do not seal it. I grew up watching my mother make this recipe in a stovetop pressure cooker. It was one of the first things I learned to make, when I was fourteen years old. It's a lot lighter than a flan, which is how I justify eating a lot of it in one sitting!

ACTIVE TIME	FUNCTION	RELEASE	TOTAL TIME
20 minutes	Sauté (Normal)	NA	45 minutes plus 4 hours chilling time

Nut-Free, Gluten-Free • 10 Ingredients or Less • SERVES 6

5 tablespoons plus ¼ cup granulated sugar

2 tablespoons water

3 large eggs

2 cups whole milk

½ teaspoon vanilla extract

Fresh berries, for garnish (optional)

1. In a medium saucepan, heat 5 tablespoons of the sugar and the water over medium heat. Allow the sugar to caramelize without stirring (it will seize up if you stir it, especially once it's started boiling). Cook until it is a deep, rich color, but do not let it burn. Quickly—and very carefully—pour the liquid caramel into a 6-inch soufflé dish that fits inside the Instant Pot.

2. In a medium bowl, whisk together the eggs, milk, remaining ¼ cup sugar, and vanilla. Pour over the top of the hardened caramel; cover the dish with foil.

3. Pour 2 cups water into the pot. Place a trivet in the pot. Place the dish on the trivet.

4. Secure the lid on the pot. Set the pressure-release valve to Venting. Select SAUTÉ/NORMAL and set a kitchen timer for 22 minutes.

5. At the end of the cooking time, insert a toothpick in the center of the custard to check for doneness. The center will be jiggly, but the toothpick should come out clean.

6. Transfer the pan to the refrigerator to chill for 4 to 6 hours.

7. When ready to serve, use a knife to loosen the edges, place a plate on top of the dish, and invert the custard onto the plate. Thump the bottom of the dish if necessary. Top with berries, if desired, and serve.

Cardamom-Carrot Pudding

The original version of this recipe uses milk solids—which you make by stirring milk over a low flame for 8 hours! Yeah, not happening in my house. I find that a combination of evaporated and condensed milk does the trick just fine. Do not cook this with the milk in the Instant Pot, as dairy sometimes separates under pressure.

ACTIVE TIME	FUNCTION	RELEASE	TOTAL TIME
10 minutes	Manual (High)	Natural + Quick	30 minutes

Egg-Free, Nut-Free, Gluten-Free · 10 Ingredients or Less · SERVES 6

4 cups chopped carrots

2 or 3 strands saffron

¾ cup water

1 (14-ounce) can sweetened condensed milk

1 (12-ounce) can evaporated milk

1 teaspoon ground cardamom

2 tablespoons chopped pistachios, for garnish (optional)

2 tablespoons salted cashews, for garnish (optional)

1. In the Instant Pot, combine the carrots, saffron, and water.

2. Secure the lid on the pot. Close the pressure-release valve. Select MANUAL and set the pot at HIGH pressure for 10 minutes. At the end of the cooking time, allow the pot to sit undisturbed for 10 minutes, then quick-release any remaining pressure. Use a potato masher to mash the carrots until roughly mashed but not puréed.

3. Stir in the condensed milk, evaporated milk, and cardamom.

4. Garnish servings with pistachios and/or cashews, if using. Serve warm or chilled.

Cassava-Ginger Pudding

Inspired by a dish I once had in Belize, this cassava pudding is an unusual gluten-free dessert with a Jell-O–like consistency. I know it may sound a bit unusual and it looks like nothing special, but it is absolutely delicious and definitely worth trying.

ACTIVE TIME	FUNCTION	RELEASE	TOTAL TIME
5 minutes	Manual (High)	Natural + Quick	35 minutes

Egg-Free, Nut-Free, Dairy-Free, Gluten-Free, Vegan • 10 Ingredients or Less • SERVES 6

Vegetable oil

1 cup cassava flour

1 (13.5-ounce) can full-fat coconut milk

½ cup granulated sugar

1 tablespoon minced fresh ginger

Sweetened whipped cream, for serving (optional)

1. Grease a 6×3-inch round baking pan with oil; set aside.

2. In a medium bowl, whisk together the cassava flour, coconut milk, sugar, and ginger. Pour the batter into the pan and cover with foil.

3. Pour 1½ cups water into the Instant Pot. Place a trivet in the pot. Place the pan on the trivet.

4. Secure the lid on the pot. Close the pressure-release valve. Select MANUAL and set the pot at HIGH pressure for 20 minutes. At the end of the cooking time, allow the pot to sit undisturbed for 10 minutes, then quick-release any remaining pressure.

5. Serve warm with whipped cream, if using.

Pumpkin Spice Bread Pudding with Maple-Cream Sauce

This dessert is "extra." It's not enough that I'm giving you a bread pudding, it's pumpkin bread pudding, and on top of that, it's pumpkin spice—and as though that weren't enough, there's that delicious sauce.

ACTIVE TIME	FUNCTION	RELEASE	TOTAL TIME
30 minutes	Manual (High)	Quick	1 hour 30 minutes

Nut-Free • SERVES 6

For the Pudding

4 tablespoons (½ stick) unsalted butter, melted, plus room-temperature butter for greasing the pan

2 large eggs

1 cup canned pumpkin purée

¾ cup heavy cream

¾ cup half-and-half

⅓ cup granulated sugar

1 teaspoon pumpkin pie spice

⅛ teaspoon kosher salt

4 cups (1-inch cubes) stale baguette or country-style bread

For the Sauce

⅓ cup pure maple syrup

1 tablespoon unsalted butter

½ cup heavy cream

½ teaspoon vanilla extract

2 tablespoons bourbon (optional)

1. **For the pudding:** Butter a 6×3-inch round baking pan.

2. In a large bowl, whisk together the melted butter, eggs, pumpkin purée, cream, half-and-half, sugar, pumpkin pie spice, and salt. Add the bread cubes and gently toss until everything is thoroughly combined and the bread has mostly soaked up the liquid. Transfer the mixture to the pan and cover with foil.

3. Pour 1½ cups water into the Instant Pot. Place a trivet in the pot. Place the pan on the trivet.

4. Secure the lid on the pot. Close the pressure-release valve. Select MANUAL and set the pot at HIGH pressure for 40 minutes. At the end of the cooking time, use a quick release to depressurize.

5. Check the pudding for doneness. If it's not set in the middle, cook for another 5 minutes. Let cool for 10 minutes.

6. **For the sauce:** Meanwhile, in a small saucepan, heat the maple syrup and butter over medium heat, stirring until the butter melts. Stir in the cream and simmer, stirring often, until the sauce has thickened, about 15 minutes. Remove the pan from heat and stir in the vanilla extract and bourbon, if using.

7. Serve the bread pudding warm with the Maple-Cream Sauce.

NOTE: For best results, use an aluminum or stainless steel pan. If you are using glass or ceramic, you may need to increase cook times.

Iced Bubble Tea

You need the sugar in this recipe not just for taste but also to keep the boba pearls from sticking to one another. If you prefer to use a sweetener other than sugar, you may not want to store this in the fridge for too long and allow the bubbles to get hard—which is just the excuse anyone needs for drinking a lot of this refreshing tea!

ACTIVE TIME	FUNCTION	RELEASE	TOTAL TIME
5 minutes	Manual (High)	Natural + Quick	30 minutes

Egg-Free, Nut-Free • 10 Ingredients or Less • SERVES 4

4 cups water

4 regular black tea or Thai black tea bags

1 cup black boba pearls

⅓ cup granulated sugar

1 cup evaporated milk

Ice cubes

1. In the Instant Pot, combine the water, tea bags, boba pearls, and sugar.

2. Secure the lid on the pot. Close the pressure-release valve. Select MANUAL and set the pot at HIGH pressure for 5 minutes. At the end of the cooking time, allow the pot to sit undisturbed for 10 minutes, then quick-release any remaining pressure. (If the pot starts to spew liquid, close the valve and try again in a minute or two.)

3. Remove the tea bags and stir in the evaporated milk.

4. Fill four glasses with ice. Pour the tea over the ice, evenly distributing the boba pearls among the glasses. Serve.

Lemongrass-Ginger Tea

Brew homemade lemongrass tea with ginger, and enjoy a cold, refreshing summer drink. Making iced tea in your Instant Pot has never been easier or more delicious.

ACTIVE TIME	FUNCTION	RELEASE	TOTAL TIME
5 minutes	Manual (High)	Natural	25 minutes plus 2 hours chilling time

Egg-Free, Nut-Free, Dairy-Free, Gluten-Free, Vegan • 10 Ingredients or Less • SERVES 6

2 cups loosely packed fresh lemongrass leaves, cut into 3- to 4-inch pieces

4 or 5 coins fresh ginger

2 tablespoons granulated sugar, or to taste

6 cups water

Fresh lemon juice

1. In the Instant Pot, combine the lemongrass leaves, ginger, sugar, and water. Stir well.

2. Secure the lid on the pot. Close the pressure-release valve. Select MANUAL and set the pot at HIGH pressure for 2 minutes. At the end of the cooking time, use a natural release to depressurize.

3. Strain the tea into a pitcher and refrigerate until chilled, at least 2 hours. Stir in lemon juice to taste.

4. Serve over ice.

SAUCES & SPICE MIXES

Ghee

I don't understand why it's so expensive to buy ghee in stores, because really, it's fairly idiot-proof to make at home. And it keeps forever on your countertop in a sealed container—or at least, it keeps as long as it takes for you to devour it... which isn't very long at our house. Note, also, that removing the milk solids makes ghee essentially dairy-free, so it's a good alternative if you're looking to avoid dairy.

MAKES	ACTIVE TIME	TOTAL TIME
2 cups	5 minutes	35 minutes

Egg-Free, Nut-Free, Dairy-Free, Gluten-Free, Low-Carb • 10 Ingredients or Less

1 pound (4 sticks) unsalted butter

1. Place the butter in a heavy-bottomed saucepan over medium-low heat. Set a timer for 20 minutes and leave it alone! Don't stir the butter or mess with it in any way. Just let it be. During this time, the water in the butter will evaporate. You'll see a light foam forming on top. It will sound like popcorn popping—but much softer.

2. At the 20-minute mark, stir the butter and raise the heat to medium-high. Cook, stirring occasionally, until the milk solids start turning brown and settling on the bottom of the pan. If you give up before this stage you are either (1) a quitter, or (b) trying to make clarified butter, not ghee.

3. Let the mixture cool a little, then strain the clear yellow liquid through a fine-mesh strainer into a jar, and you're done. (Discard the browned milk solids.)

4. Seal the jar tightly with the lid. You can store the ghee on your countertop almost indefinitely, as long as you keep it sealed and use a clean spoon each time you dig into it.

Niter Kibbeh

Your house will smell so good when you make this! Niter kibbeh is clarified butter with aromatics and spices in it. It's easy to make—and even easier to eat on vegetables, in stews, and everywhere else where you might use ghee or butter.

MAKES	ACTIVE TIME	TOTAL TIME
1½ cups	10 minutes	40 minutes

Egg-Free, Nut-Free, Gluten-Free, Dairy-Free, Vegan, Low-Carb • 10 Ingredients or Less

1 pound (4 sticks) unsalted butter or 1 (14-ounce) jar coconut oil

1 yellow onion, chopped

4 cloves garlic, minced

1 tablespoon minced fresh ginger

1½ teaspoons coarsely ground black pepper

1 teaspoon cardamom seeds

1 teaspoon fenugreek seeds

½ teaspoon cumin seeds

½ teaspoon ground turmeric

1 or 2 Indian cinnamon sticks (cassia bark) or ½ regular cinnamon stick, broken into small pieces

4 whole cloves

1. In a medium saucepan, combine the butter, onion, garlic, ginger, black pepper, cardamom seeds, fenugreek seeds, cumin seeds, turmeric, cinnamon sticks, and cloves. Bring to a simmer over medium-low heat. Allow to simmer for about 30 minutes, until the bubbles that rise to the top appear clear and the mixture is no longer milky.

2. Place a fine-mesh strainer over a heatproof jar (such as a 2-cup canning jar). Strain the mixture into the jar; discard the solids. Seal the jar tightly with the lid. You can store the niter kibbeh on your countertop almost indefinitely, as long as you keep it sealed and use a clean spoon each time you dig into it.

NOTE: For a vegan version, use coconut oil instead of butter.

Harissa

Many harissa recipes use tomatoes or peppers. I prefer my paste to be straight-up spice. Taste it once and you will find a million different uses for this lovely, spicy, versatile mix.

MAKES	ACTIVE TIME	TOTAL TIME
1 cup	5 minutes	10 minutes

Egg-Free, Nut-Free, Dairy-Free, Gluten-Free, Vegan, Low-Carb • 10 Ingredients or Less

½ cup vegetable oil

6 cloves garlic, minced

2 tablespoons smoked paprika

1 tablespoon ground coriander

1 tablespoon ground cumin

1 teaspoon ground caraway

1 teaspoon kosher salt

½ to 1 teaspoon cayenne pepper

1. In a medium microwave-safe bowl, combine the oil, garlic, paprika, coriander, cumin, caraway, salt, and cayenne pepper. Microwave on high for 1 minute, stirring halfway through the cooking time. You can also heat this on the stovetop until the oil is hot and bubbling.

2. Cool completely. Store in an airtight container in the refrigerator for up to 1 month.

RECIPE	PAGE	EGG-FREE	NUT-FREE	DAIRY-FREE	GLUTEN-FREE	VEGAN	LOW-CARB	30 MINUTES OR LESS	10 INGREDIENTS OR LESS
CREAMED GREEN BEANS AND MUSHROOMS	38	X	X		X		X	X	X
COCONUT GREEN BEANS	39	X	X	X	X	X	X	X	X
GREEK-STYLE GREEN BEANS AND POTATOES	41	X	X	X	X	X		X	X
UNSTUFFED GRAPE LEAVES	42	X		X	X	X			X
BUTTERNUT-GINGER SOUP	43	X	X	X	X	X			X
GARLIC-PARMESAN SPAGHETTI SQUASH	44	X			X		X		X
VEGETABLE CURRY WITH TOFU	47	X	X	X		X			X
TEX-MEX CORN PUDDING	48		X						X
CAJUN CORN CHOWDER	52	X	X	X	X				X
BUTTER "CHICKEN" WITH SOY CURLS	53	X	X	X	X	X	X		
JAMAICAN MIXED VEGETABLE CURRY	57	X	X	X	X	X			X
BEET AND LENTIL SALAD	60	X	X	X	X	X			X
CREAMY BEET-YOGURT DIP WITH DILL AND GARLIC	61	X	X						X
MINTY PEAS	64	X	X	X	X	X		X	X
SUMMER SQUASH COUSCOUS	67	X	X	X		X		X	
SWEET-AND-SPICY GLAZED BRUSSELS SPROUTS	68	X	X	X	X	X		X	X
BRAISED CABBAGE PASTA	71	X	X	X		X			X
TURMERIC-SPICED CABBAGE AND POTATOES	72	X	X	X	X	X		X	X
SWEET-AND-SOUR RED CABBAGE	74	X	X	X	X	X		X	X
UNSTUFFED CABBAGE ROLLS	75	X	X	X		X			X
SMOKY BRAISED KALE WITH TOMATOES	76	X	X	X	X	X	X		X
TANGY OKRA AND TOMATOES	77	X	X	X	X	X	X	X	X
KIMCHI STEW	79	X	X	X		X	X	X	
SUMMER VEGETABLE SOUP	80	X	X		X	X	X	X	X
HEARTY GREENS AND POTATO STEW	83	X	X	X	X	X			
EGGPLANT–TOMATO STEW WITH CHICKPEAS AND FRESH BASIL	86	X	X	X	X	X	X		X
COCONUT-CABBAGE SOUP	87	X	X	X	X	X	X	X	
TORTELLINI SOUP WITH KALE	91	X	X					X	X
SICILIAN SWEET-AND-SOUR EGGPLANT	94	X	X	X	X	X	X		X
SMOKY EGGPLANT DIP	95	X	X	X		X			X
EGGPLANT PARMIGIANA PASTA	97	X	X						
HOT-AND-SOUR SOUP	98		X	X	X		X		X
MUSHROOM STROGANOFF	99	X	X					X	X
MUSHROOM-MASCARPONE PASTA	100	X	X						X
BUTTERY WHIPPED POTATOES WITH CABBAGE	102	X	X		X				X
SPICY COCONUT-CHICKPEA CURRY	113	X	X	X	X	X			X
CHICKPEAS IN SPICY TOMATO SAUCE WITH BROWN RICE	114	X	X	X	X	X			
SPICED RED LENTILS	118	X	X	X	X	X			X
TANGY MUNG BEAN STEW	119	X	X	X	X	X			
TEXAS CAVIAR	121	X	X	X	X	X			X
CHIPOTLE CHILI WITH ZUCCHINI, CORN, AND FIRE-ROASTED TOMATOES	124	X	X	X	X	X			
PINTO POZOLE STEW	125	X	X	X	X	X			X
CHILI-SPICED PINTO BEANS IN RED SAUCE	128	X	X	X	X	X			X
PEANUT-SAUCED VEGGIES AND BLACK-EYED PEAS	129	X		X	X	X			X
COLLARD GREENS AND RED BEAN STEW	130	X	X	X	X	X			X
BLACK BEAN SOUP	131	X	X	X	X	X			
MIXED-BEAN BURRITO BOWLS	134	X	X		X				
SMOKY RED BEAN–VEGETABLE STEW	135	X	X	X	X	X			X
CUMIN-SCENTED BLACK BEANS AND RICE	138	X	X	X	X	X			X
BLACK BEAN TORTILLA SOUP	139	X	X	X	X	X			X
HARISSA BEAN STEW	140	X	X	X	X	X			X
CREAMY GREEK GIGANTES BEANS	143	X	X	X		X			X

RECIPE	PAGE	EGG-FREE	NUT-FREE	DAIRY-FREE	GLUTEN-FREE	VEGAN	LOW-CARB	30 MINUTES OR LESS	10 INGREDIENTS OR LESS
LEMONY LIMA–NAVY BEAN SOUP	144	X	X	X	X	X			X
BOSTON BAKED BEANS	147	X	X	X					X
SIMPLE ADZUKI BEANS AND STICKY RICE	148	X	X	X	X	X			X
WHITE BEAN–POTATO SOUP WITH SAUERKRAUT	151	X	X	X	X	X			X
CAJUN RED BEANS	152	X	X	X	X	X			
LEBANESE LENTILS AND RICE	163	X	X	X	X	X			X
GREEK SPINACH AND RICE	164	X	X	X	X	X			X
JEWELED COCONUT RICE	167	X	X	X	X	X			X
MEXICAN RED RICE	168	X	X	X	X	X			X
CUMIN-CARDAMOM RICE WITH PEAS AND CARROTS	171	X	X	X	X	X			X
CURRIED VEGETABLE RICE	172	X	X	X	X	X			X
SESAME-GINGER RICE PORRIDGE	173	X	X	X	X	X			X
COCONUT RED BEANS AND RICE	174	X	X	X	X	X			X
RICE AND LENTIL PORRIDGE	175	X	X	X	X				X
FARRO RISOTTO WITH BUTTERNUT SQUASH AND GREEN ONIONS	177	X	X						X
FARRO-BEAN SALAD	178	X	X	X		X			X
KASHA PILAF WITH CRANBERRIES, KALE, AND TOASTED WALNUTS	181	X		X	X	X			X
CRANBERRY-MILLET PORRIDGE	184	X	X	X	X	X			X
SIMPLE WILD RICE PILAF	185	X	X	X	X	X			X
CILANTRO-LIME MILLET PILAF	188	X	X	X	X	X			X
CINNAMON-SPICED BULGUR PILAF WITH RED LENTILS	189	X	X	X		X			X
MUSHROOM-BARLEY PILAF	191	X	X	X		X			X
COUSCOUS PILAF WITH FETA AND RED ONION	192	X	X					X	X
EGG LOAF	196		X	X	X		X	X	X
EGG CUPS	197		X		X		X		X
ITALIAN GREENS AND EGGS	200		X		X		X		X
HOMEMADE PANEER	201	X	X		X		X		X
BROCCOLI AND CHEESE FRITTATA	202		X		X		X		X
ASPARAGUS GRIBICHE	203		X	X	X		X	X	X
SPINACH AND CHEESE STRATA	204		X						X
HOT FUDGE PUDDING CAKE	209		X						X
BOX MIX BLUEBERRY CAKE	210		X						X
STEAMED SPONGE CAKE	213		X	X					X
MANGO CHEESECAKE	214		X		X				X
COCONUT RICE PUDDING WITH SAFFRON, RAISINS, AND CASHEWS	217	X			X				X
EIGHT TREASURES RICE SOUP	219	X		X		X			X
SWEET RED BEAN SOUP	220	X	X	X	X	X			X
MIXED FRUIT KESARI	221	X	X	X		X			X
APPLE-QUINOA PORRIDGE	222	X	X		X			X	X
BOSTON BROWN BREAD	225		X						X
CHESS PIE CUSTARD	226		X		X				X
CARDAMOM YOGURT	227	X	X		X				X
CARAMEL CUSTARD	228		X		X				X
CARDAMOM-CARROT PUDDING	231	X	X		X			X	X
CASSAVA-GINGER PUDDING	232	X	X	X	X	X			X
PUMPKIN SPICE BREAD PUDDING WITH MAPLE-CREAM SAUCE	233		X						
ICED BUBBLE TEA	234	X	X					X	X
LEMONGRASS-GINGER TEA	236	X	X	X	X	X			X
GHEE	240	X	X	X	X		X		X
NITER KIBBEH	241	X	X	X	X	X	X		X
HARISSA	242	X	X	X	X	X	X	X	X

INDEX

Note: Page references in *italics* indicate photographs.

P

Paneer, Homemade, 201

Paprika
  Smoky Braised Kale with Tomatoes, 76
  Smoky Red Bean–Vegetable Stew, 135, *136–37*

Pasta. *See also* Couscous
  Braised Cabbage, *70,* 71
  Eggplant Parmigiana, *96,* 97
  Mushroom-Mascarpone, 100, *101*
  Mushroom Stroganoff, 99
  Tortellini Soup with Kale, *90,* 91

Peanut-Sauced Veggies and Black-Eyed Peas, 129

Peas
  Braised Cabbage Pasta, *70,* 71
  and Carrots, Cumin-Cardamom Rice with, *170,* 171
  Couscous Pilaf with Feta and Red Onion, 192, *193*
  Curried Vegetable Rice, 172
  Minty, 64, *65*

Peas, Black-Eyed
  Farro-Bean Salad, 178, *179*
  Texas Caviar, *120,* 121
  and Veggies, Peanut-Sauced, 129

Peppers
  Black Bean Soup, 131
  Broccoli and Cheese Frittata, 202
  Cajun Corn Chowder, *50–51,* 52
  Coconut-Cabbage Soup, 87, *88–89*
  Cumin-Scented Black Beans and Rice, 138

Curried Vegetable Rice, 172
Eggplant-Tomato Stew with Chickpeas and Fresh Basil, *84–85,* 86
Italian Greens and Eggs, *198–99,* 200
Jamaican Mixed Vegetable Curry, *56,* 57
Minty Peas, 64, *65*
Mixed-Bean Burrito Bowls, *132–33,* 134
Smoky Red Bean–Vegetable Stew, 135, *136–37*
Vegetable Curry with Tofu, *46,* 47

Pilaf
  Bulgur, Cinnamon-Spiced, with Red Lentils, 189
  Couscous, with Feta and Red Onion, 192, *193*
  Kasha, with Cranberries, Kale, and Toasted Walnuts, *180,* 181
  Millet, Cilantro-Lime, 188
  Mushroom-Barley, *190,* 191
  Wild Rice, Simple, 185, *186–87*

Pine nuts
  Cinnamon-Spiced Bulgur Pilaf with Red Lentils, 189
  Sicilian Sweet-and-Sour Eggplant, *92–93,* 94
  Unstuffed Grape Leaves, 42

Pinto Pozole Stew, 125, *126–27*

PIP (pot-in-pot) cooking, 24

Porridge
  Apple-Quinoa, 222, *223*
  Cranberry-Millet, *182–83,* 184
  Rice, Sesame-Ginger, 173
  Rice and Lentil, 175

Potato(es)
  Buttery Whipped, with Cabbage, 102, *103*
  and Cabbage, Turmeric-Spiced, 72, *73*
  Cajun Corn Chowder, *50–51,* 52
  and Green Beans, Greek-Style, *40,* 41
  and Hearty Greens Stew, *82,* 83
  Jamaican Mixed Vegetable Curry, *56,* 57
  Peanut-Sauced Veggies and Black-Eyed Peas, 129
  –White Bean Soup with Sauerkraut, *150,* 151

Pozole Pinto Stew, 125, *126–27*

Pressure cook/manual button, 26

Pudding
  Bread, Pumpkin Spice, with Maple-Cream Sauce, 233
  Cardamom-Carrot, *230,* 231
  Cassava-Ginger, 232
  Rice, Coconut, with Saffron, Raisins, and Cashews, 217
  Tex-Mex Corn, 48, *49*

Pulses, defined, 106

Pumpkin
  Jamaican Mixed Vegetable Curry, *56,* 57
  Spice Bread Pudding with Maple-Cream Sauce, 233

QPR (quick pressure release), 24–25, 34

Quinoa-Apple Porridge, 222, *223*

R

S

Cook more healthy and delicious recipes in your Instant Pot!

AUTHORIZED BY INSTANT POT®

Instant Pot® Miracle

HEALTHY COOKBOOK

More than 100 Easy Healthy Meals for Your Favorite Kitchen Device

URVASHI PITRE

BIBIMBAP

WHITE BEAN SAUSAGE SOUP

CLASSIC POT ROAST